Of
Danish
Ways

Of Danish Ways

By

INGEBORG S. MacHAFFIE and MARGARET A. NIELSEN

Illustrated by Henning Jensen

PERENNIAL LIBRARY

Harper & Row, Publishers
New York, Cambridge, Philadelphia, San Francisco
London, Mexico City, São Paulo, Singapore, Sydney

Library of Congress Cataloging in Publication Data

MacHaffie, Ingeborg S.
   Of Danish ways.

   Reprint. Originally published: Minneapolis, Minn. : Dillon Press, 1976 (Heritage books)
   Bibliography: p.
   Includes index.
   1. Denmark—Civilization. I. Nielsen, Margaret A.
II. Title.

[DL131.M19 1984]   948.9   83-48367
ISBN 0-06-092318-0

92 93 94 95 MPC 10 9 8 7 6 5 4 3 2 1

CONTENTS

FOREWORD

Have you visited Denmark? Do you plan to do so? Copenhagen, the city of laughter, is one place you must be sure to see. It is one of the most fascinating cities in the world. But don't stop there, or you will get a very lopsided view of Denmark. You will miss the country's wide beaches and charming islands, the picturesque villages and lovely beech woods, the busy ferries and bustling provincial cities. In fact, you will miss more than half of Denmark if you visit only Copenhagen.

Denmark is such a small country—scarcely the size of the Willamette Valley in Oregon, with a population less than half that of greater Los Angeles. Would you believe, then, that at one time the Danes owned great expanses of territory—England, Germany, Sweden, Norway, as well as Iceland and Greenland?

But Denmark, although small in size, has had a great impact upon the face of the globe. Perhaps the Danes have been blessed by the smallness of their nation. The country's size has enabled them to observe the world as through a telescope—to obtain from that vantage point a good, clear perspective of the needs and problems of society. Adding their own ingenuity and special talents to this perspective, the Danes have come up with many contributions and solutions to the world's problems.

Denmark is a place of rich and romantic culture—from the sagas, ballads, and stone carvings of old, to the most modern forms of music, art, and literature.

Denmark is a land of inventions. She has a whimsical flair for inventing practical gadgets, like the recent automatic bottle return device that receives, sorts, and records, then dispenses a receipt.

Denmark is a monarchy, with a popular queen at the helm. And yet Denmark is one of the most staunchly democratic nations in the world, dedicated to the philosophy that every citizen has a right to be heard and a right to be cared for, from cradle to grave.

Even though her politics rests in the hands of as many as seven active political parties, Denmark is characterized by considerable uniformity—ethnically, economically, even geographically. There are, significantly, no mountains, just as there are no really poor people and few who are really rich. There are no slums.

More and more visitors are discovering the attractions of this peaceable, progressive land, although few are acquainted with the many diverse features of her culture, her industry, and her politics. Even Denmark's intriguing history and charming, unique customs escape the attention of the casual tourist.

A single book cannot possibly include all the details of Denmark's special qualities and many achievements, but this small volume has covered an amazing amount of informational material and created a delightful composite picture of Denmark and the Danes—past and present.

The two sister authors, born of Danish parents and reared in a Danish environment, speak the Danish language fluently. They have visited and resided in Denmark a number of times. Although their versatile and wide educational backgrounds have led them into completely different and distinguished teaching careers, their interest in their ancestral land has never diminished. In fact, it has been enhanced even more through their extensive research.

For all who wish to have a fascinating overview and a deeper appreciation of Denmark and Danish ways, the book is filled with gems of information, excelled only by the evident enthusiasm of the authors for a country that is, indeed, a lovable, as well as lovely, *dejligt,* land.

HARVEY BENSON
Danish Consul, Portland, Oregon

SKAGEN

FREDERIKSHAVN

AALBORG

THISTED

MORS

HOLSTEBRO

SILKEBORG   EBELTOFT

HERNING   AARHUS

JUTLAND

HORSENS   ELSINORE

ROSKILDE   COPENHAGEN

ESBJERG   ZEALAND

ODENSE   RINGSTED

RIBE   FUNEN

VORDINGBORG

DENMARK

BORNHOLM

PROLOGUE

HANS CHRISTIAN ANDERSEN, beloved Danish author, writes of his homeland in this way:*

Between the Baltic Sea and the North Sea lies an old swan's nest. It is called "Danmark," and in it are born swans whose names shall never die.

In antiquity, a swan flock flew from its nest over the Alps to Italy's green plains, where living was pleasant. [The swan flock was known as the Lombardians.]

Another group with shining feathers and trusting eyes swooped down toward Byzantine and established itself around the emperor's throne, spreading large white wings as shields to protect him. [These swans earned the name of Varangians and were bodyguards of the Byzantine emperor in the twelfth century.]

From the coast of France came a cry of fear, as bloody swans, with fire under their wings, attacked from the north, and the people prayed, "Deliver us, God, from the wild Normans." [These swans were the Vikings.]

On England's fresh green coasts by the open sea stood a Danish swan with a three-tiered king's crown upon its head, extending a golden scepter over the land. [Canute the Great was king of Denmark, Sweden, and Norway as well as England.]

And the heathens fell on their knees on the Pomeranian coast, as the Danish swans came with the cross's flag and drawn sword. [Valdemar II became sovereign over Rugen and Estonia in the 1200s.]

"That was in the ancient days," you say.

Well, also, nearer our own time, mighty swans have flown from their nest. A swan, with strong wings beating, separated the thick fog, and the starry heaven became clearer. It appeared suddenly to be nearer to the earth. [This was the astronomer Tycho Brahe.]

"Yes, but it was then, not today!" you say.

Now we have seen more swans flying in glorious flight. One allowed his wing to glide over the strings of a golden harp which rang through the north. Norway's fjords were lifted higher in the ancient sunlight. The wind blew through the evergreen and beech trees, and Norse gods appeared in the deep dark woods. [This was the Norwegian composer Edvard Grieg.]

We saw a swan strike with its wing against a mountain of marble, splintering the lovely stone, and from its fragments beautiful figures were shaped in the brightest day. People around the world lifted their heads to see these marvelous works. [These wings belonged to the sculptor Bertel Thorvaldsen.]

We saw yet another swan spin threads of wisdom, which now reach around the world from shore to shore as the word flies at lightning speed through all lands. [This was the philosopher Søren Kierkegaard.]

God holds dear this old swan's nest between the Baltic and the North Sea. Let mighty birds come through the air to break it asunder: it shall not happen! The young cygnets will place themselves in a ring on the edge of the nest, as we have seen, and bearing their young breasts as shields, give their life's blood in defending the nest with beak and claw.

Hundreds of years will pass, and swans will fly from their nest to be seen and heard around the world before that time comes, when at last in spirit and in truth it can be said, "It is the last swan, the last song coming from the swan's nest."

*Translated by Ingeborg MacHaffie from "The Swan's Nest."

Archbishop Absalon, the founder of Copenhagen

CHAPTER 1

A LITTLE COUNTRY WITH A BIG SPIRIT

SMILING DENMARK! Home of the Danes, a happy people in a delightful country!

To learn about Denmark, you must meet the Danes,

> whose ingredients for living are food, song, humor, and sociability,
>
> whose ways of friendliness, helpfulness, and hospitality are their weapons for peace,
>
> who have neither too much nor too little,
>
> who are proud of their country and its heritage of social concern,
>
> who are hardy, literate, broadminded, and enterprising.

The Danes *are* Denmark, smiling Denmark!

How did the country come to be named *Danmark*? You may have heard that the name means "field of the Danes." And the word *mark* does mean "field." But where did the term *Dan* originate? Which came first, the people or the name?

Denmark may have derived its name from one of the first kings that ruled over the many kingdoms of that ancient land. One of the oldest manuscripts found in Denmark says, "Dan is the name of the first king of Denmark." In the same handwriting the notation continues, "When Dan had driven the enemies out of Jutland, he assembled his men to confer with them concerning a name for his kingdom. One of the oldest warriors arose and burst out, 'You are Dan! Your kingdom shall be called Danmark, and this name shall exist as long as the world shall stand!' "

True or not, the story of Dan may be more believable than a myth concerning the origin of the country itself, which is depicted in an imposing statue in Copenhagen—that of the goddess Gefion and her three sons who were turned into oxen. Gefion and her sons had to carve out the land of Denmark in a twenty-four-hour period!

Whatever the truth is, the name *Danmark* has its origin well over a thousand years ago, and the name, as well as the kingdom, is the oldest in Europe.

Denmark, the southernmost country of all Scandinavia, is composed of the peninsula of Jutland, which extends north from Germany; two main islands, Zealand and Funen; and about five hundred other islands, more than one hundred of which are inhabited. Greenland, the largest island in the world, is also a Danish possession. So, too, are the seventeen Faroe Islands, located two hundred and fifty miles northwest of Scotland.

Exclusive of Greenland and the Faroes, the entire area of Denmark itself is only 16,619 square miles, or about twice the size of Massachusetts.

The position of the country, between the North Sea and the Baltic, in the direct pathway of shipping from Scandinavia to central Europe, has been to its advantage from earliest times. Ideas as well as items of trade have come in from every direction, bringing the Danes not only good business but also a diversity of cultural influences.

When you are in Denmark, you are almost always conscious of the sea. Gently rolling sand dunes, covered with limed grass that checks the shifting sand, form sheltering shoulders on the bleak western coast of Jutland. The giant waves of the North Sea push steadily against the extreme tip of the peninsula. At one point, Råbjerg Mile near the Skaw (the uppermost tip of Jutland), the north wind blows so fiercely that a 130-foot bank of sand is being moved eastward at the rate of ten feet a year!

With a coastline of about five thousand miles and numerous ports and inlets, the country naturally developed sea-related occupations—from the early Viking expeditions in the ninth century to mercantile trade and shipbuilding in the twentieth century.

On the long western and northern coastlines facing the North Sea, as well as on all the islands, the Danes have earned their livelihood from fishing for hundreds of years. The main fishing ports are Esbjerg, Hirtshals, Hvide Sande, and Thyborøn. Hvide Sande, which means "white sands," is a long man-made spit of sand sheltering the inlet at Ringkøbing from the North Sea.

The largest cities and principal towns in Denmark are situated on the coast or other waterways, where early settlers built fortifications or developed trading or fishing ports. Largest of these cities, besides Copenhagen, are Århus, Odense, Ålborg, Esbjerg, and Randers.

Denmark's weather is surprisingly moderate for a country with a northern latitude of fifty-four to fifty-eight degrees. Its winter temperature ranges from 20 to 40 degrees Fahrenheit, and the summer heat rarely goes above 70. February is usually the coldest month, with a mean temperature of 32; July, the warmest, with about 62. The changing air streams blowing across large masses of cold North Atlantic waters may at times produce extremely cold weather, and the lowest recorded temperature was —23, a record established in 1940. The highest temperature ever recorded was 96.5.

Snow usually falls only four or five days a month during the winter. It is light and does not accumulate to great depths. Occasionally, however, severe snowstorms do occur, producing as much as eighteen to twenty-four inches of snow.

The mean annual rainfall in Denmark is 23.5 inches, but the low-lying coastal areas in Jutland and Funen usually receive more than that. Rain is intermittent the year around, but, unfortunately, rainfall does not always coincide with the farmers' needs.

Geologically, much of Denmark, especially Jutland, is a product of glacial action. A large area of western Jutland was laid down as glacial morraine deposits some forty thousand years ago. The soil, made up of clay, sand, chalk, and limestone, is poor in essential plant foods, such as nitrogen, potassium, and sulfates, although it is rich in calcium.

Only a poor grade of coal is found in Denmark, and a limited supply of energy poses a serious problem, since the country depends entirely on other countries for its fuel, including oil and petroleum. Oil, petroleum, and solid fuels constitute 72 percent of the nation's imports, and these goods are supplied mainly by Great Britain, Germany, and the United States. Plans are rapidly being made for further exploration of fuel sources, such as those on the Danish continental shelf of the North Sea, where natural gas and oil have been found in a few drillings. Energy from water power is obtained from Norway and Sweden. The construction of nuclear plants is being contemplated for several sites in the country.

For agricultural purposes, soil of the type found in most of Denmark is dependent on favorable climate, fertilizer, and adequate cultivation to become productive. However, in eastern Jutland, the land is more fertile. The people living in that area seem to be more relaxed and easygoing, possibly because they do not have to work so hard to prepare and improve the land!

Three-fourths of the total land area of Denmark is devoted to agriculture, and of the 140,000 farms in Denmark today, 62 percent are in cultivation with feed and grain crops. About 10 percent of the farming area is planted to grass for hay, but oats, rye, wheat, and root crops are also grown. Much of the land is planted in cattle beets. These huge beets, high in sugar and protein content, can be seen in the fields in the fall, ready to be chopped for feeding dairy cattle. Ninety percent of the farmers' gross income comes from animal products—butter, cheese, bacon, beef, poultry, and eggs.

One of the most eye-catching things on the Danish landscape is the typical Danish *gaard,* or cluster of farm buildings. The buildings are arranged in a joined U shape, with the farmhouse, cow barn, pig stall, and machine shed all built around a court. Everything is so neat and clean inside and out that one can scarcely distinguish house from barn. The buildings are whitewashed every two years, and the thickly thatched or tiled roofs seem to last for years.

"Where are your fine pink and white pigs?" asked a visitor when he didn't see them in the barnyard or the fields.

"Oh, they live inside the barn, where they can be kept clean," replied the farmer.

Half of the Danish farms are small, less than twenty-five acres in size. Although the trend is toward larger farms and more mechanization, the small farmer still plays a valuable role in the economy. It is only within the last few years that farming has become second in importance to industry as a source of national income.

There are no mountains in this land of farms. The highest point in Denmark—at Yding Skov in eastern Jutland—

is only 585 feet above sea level. But the Danes do claim to have a "mountain," called *Himmelbjerget,* or "Heaven's Mountain." It has an elevation of 490 feet and is located in the lake region of central Jutland. From the highest point of this landmark the view is magnificent. The beech trees seem to spill their green and yellow colors across the golden grains of the fields, and Århus Cathedral and the spires of Viborg Cathedral are visible in the distance on a clear day.

Danish towns, most of them dating back to the Middle Ages, have sprung up near harbors, as previously mentioned, or around cathedrals and monasteries. Of the twenty-three hundred churches in Denmark, about eighteen hundred were built before the fourteenth century. The neat white church, often dominating the landscape and nearly always shading a garden-like cemetery, is a common landmark of the village. Churches with the typical stepped-roof architecture, which dates back to the 1700s, are remarkably preserved, even to the delicate fresco paintings on the interiors. Quaint and romantic, the towns are nearly all steeped in fascinating history and legends, reflected in their centuries-old houses or their inns (*kroer*), in their cobblestone streets, or in their outlying *gaards,* some of them nearly five hundred years old.

If you were to characterize the three largest areas of Denmark—Jutland, Funen, and Zealand—you might describe Jutland as the most widely varied and historically interesting, the island of Funen as the most picturesque and idyllic, and Zealand as the most exciting.

The peninsula of Jutland, by far the largest area of Denmark, is probably the most interesting and delightful to those who enjoy the contrasts of the past and the present. Villages, manor farms, churches, castles, and offshore islands yield fascinating tales of Denmark's heritage. They comprise a veritable fairyland of artifacts and adventure, architecture and anecdotes.

On the northeastern coast of Jutland, for example, lie the manor farms of Djursland and Mols, where heaths and marshlands alternate with woods and green fields, and a medieval country church is usually prominent on the horizon. Unique rolling mounds and cliff formations extend down to the fine sandy beaches and fishing harbors. Ebeltoft, located in the picturesque eastern tip of this area, is one of Denmark's quaintest and best preserved old villages. Its town hall (the smallest in Europe), its tiny houses, its ancient, authentic inns—all give to the town an old-world flavor.

Second in size only to Copenhagen is the city of Århus, located on the Lillebelt Strait on the eastern coast of Jutland. It is a major port, with a population of about two hundred thousand, that still retains much old-world atmosphere. As early as the year 928, the city was the site of a bishopric, and several of the oldest churches still stand, including the famous Århus Cathedral, which dates back to 1201, the year the first stone was laid.

Other Jutland towns and a few of their noteworthy attractions include: Ålborg, which is famous for *akvavit*—the strong Danish brandy—and for the Jens Bang (1623) Manor, the grandest patrician Renaissance mansion of the north; Viborg, which is the site of an ancient and beautiful cathedral; Holstebro, where a modern religious and cultural center attracts performing musicians, actors, and artists; and Silkeborg, where a museum houses the Tollund Man and an excursion boat with a waterwheel awaits passengers for a water tour to Himmelbjerget.

Off the southern tip of Jutland, the island of Als offers diverse recreational activities and excursions. Rich in tradition, the island shows through its customs and atmosphere that it is distinctly Danish. From Sønderborg, the leading town on Als, one can go by car or boat along the fjords between the islands and the mainland, enjoying such sights as prehistoric burial mounds, Sandbjerg Castle, old fishing villages, and the islands, woods, and beaches.

It is said that Hans Christian Andersen, when visiting the Duke of Slesvig at Augustenborg Castle on Als in the 1840s, wrote his story "The Snow Queen" under one of the huge lime trees there in the park, which is now open to the public.

The island of Aerø, to the east of Als, has been called the "pearl of the archipelago" and is one of the loveliest spots to be found in Denmark. Attractions abound there also, among which the collection of five hundred models of ships in bottles is most often mentioned, although one may prefer to see the garden of the Inn of Bregninge, or one of the most beautiful Scandinavian triptychs in the Church of Bregninge.

The city of Odense, on the island of Funen, is the third largest in the kingdom. It is most noted as the birthplace of Hans Christian Andersen. Near Odense is also an outdoor museum—a reproduction of a village from earliest times. A burial ground of Viking graves found at Nonnebakken, one section of the city, is one of the most interesting of the Danish archeological discoveries.

Funen has more flower gardens and woods than any other part of Denmark. The lovely old manor estates, small villages with low half-timbered houses, and picturesque farm scenes have been the subject for many paintings. One of the best preserved of ancient Danish towns is Fåborg, whose town charter dates from the year 1251. Northeast of Fåborg are the beautiful low hills called *Svanninge Bakker,* from the heights of which you can view the many smaller islands south of Funen.

Of the approximately 5 million people inhabiting Denmark, half live on the island of Zealand—an area of about three thousand square miles—with 1.5 million living in and around the capital city of Copenhagen (*København*), major port on the direct sea route to the Baltic.

To most persons outside of Denmark, the fascinating city of Copenhagen *is* Denmark. The fun, the shops, the variety of cultural attractions, and the charming atmosphere appeal to the pleasure-seeking tourist and seem to reinforce any preconceived ideas of the country.

The weathered green copper roofs of the city tell a tale covering five hundred years of history; its many Renaissance buildings date back to the reign of King Christian IV in the 1400s. The oldest stock exchange building in the world, called *Børsen*, proudly flaunts its distinctive dragon's tail spire. *Børsen* stands at the waterfront of this ancient "port of trade," which *København* literally means.

In Copenhagen's imposing castles and ancient cathedrals, in its fishmarket on Gammel Strand at Nyhavn, you feel wrapped in an old-world setting. Yet, strolling up the wide shopping street of Vesterbrogade, you will encounter the ultimate in modern design and culture in elegant department stores and exclusive shops, which feature items of high quality, such as fashions, Danish modern furniture, and exquisite china or silver.

Although Strøget—perhaps the *original* pedestrian shopping mall—does not exactly resemble the Champs Élysées, Copenhagen has nevertheless been called the Paris of Scandinavia. Intriguing little specialty shops alternate with nightclubs to provide everyone a wide choice of attractions.

Tivoli, a sparkling jewel of entertainment set in the center of the city's shopping ring, is open from May until mid-September to fun-loving Danes and tourists. This festive

amusement garden offers professional performances of classical symphony and pantomime-ballet to the most sophisti-
cated, and "fun" activities—such as shooting galleries, merry-
go-rounds, and a roller coaster—to everyone. A profusion of
colored lights, flowers, fountains, waterfalls, sidewalk restaurants, and night firework displays creates a carnival atmosphere of merrymaking.

Yes, this buzzing metropolis offers a bit of everything to
everyone's taste—in varieties of food as well as diver-
sion. Restaurants aplenty bid you forget your diets and
relish your repast, from soup such as you've never tasted
before, to flaky Danish pastry that is artistic as well as delicious. A Danish sandwich is an attractive, satisfying meal,
and you may forget completely your accustomed lunch of a
hamburger and french fries!

The eastern coast of Zealand is a picturesque and interesting section of Denmark, with fine sandy beaches, lakes,
woods, and many popular resorts. So varied are the entice-
ments of the scenic coastal stretch extending thirty miles
north of Copenhagen that it is often given the colorful name
of the Danish Riviera. Museums, castles, art galleries, outdoor theaters, as well as resorts and scenery—all these make
it a region of superlative attractiveness.

In southern Zealand are found moat-surrounded castles,
historic inns, twelfth-century churches, and market towns
with remarkably preserved half-timbered houses, such as at
Køge, Naestved, and Slagelse.

In a tour through the beautiful and historic sights of Denmark's major areas, you will see that the face of Denmark
has a contrasting side—a marked modernization of its urban
and suburban environments. With the growth of the population, the need for more adequate housing has increased, and,
as a result, an expansive program of building has changed

the scene. In the outskirts of the cities, large complexes of six- to ten-story apartment houses loom starkly bare and grim against the sky, like the hands of a clock testifying to the facts of the times—industrialization and need. However, gardens and bright drapes do provide color for the stone-gray flats, and open spaces are left for recreation and play.

Also throughout the entire country, in the proximity of the larger towns, compact family dwellings have sprung up in amazing numbers—some single-storied, some double-storied, some semi-detached—in clustered arrangements with individual or shared garden space. Various novel architectural designs are appearing, true to the innovative ideas of Danish architects.

A common sight near metropolitan centers is a mechanical crane of skyscraper height looming far above the horizon. With almost shocking speed, it erects rectangular, circular, or diagonal structures that provide an amazing contrast to the traditional picture of Denmark. The character of the new design will yet become engraved as a pattern on the Danish landscape as part of the Danes' cultural ingenuity in an era of change.

And what of the people who inhabit this land? The typical Dane generally is thought to be fair-haired or sandy-haired —round-faced, ruddy-complexioned, and smiling—though dark-skinned Danes and mixed colorings are often seen.

In temperament, the Danish people are known to be jovial, friendly, hospitable, and emotionally warm. They enjoy a good time and are very sociable, but they are also sincere, law abiding, and industrious. They live in cozy homes, enjoy television with a fervor, and are concerned with children, recreation, food, and taxes! They express their respect for the royal family and *Dannebrog,* the Danish flag. In fact, the red-and-white pennant is a meaningful emblem, daily seen flying high in front of public buildings, stores, and homes. On any special holiday—of which there are many— or on the birthday of any member of the family, *Dannebrog* may be flown.

Dannebrog is not only respected, it is also universally beloved. It represents the land the Danes love, the toil that went into building their country, and the spirit that has held the people together in a common bond. Numerous songs and lyrics have been written in honor of the flag, expressing the Danes' deepest feelings for this emblem. These tributes have served to strengthen human ties and patriotic loyalty during difficult times. Symbolizing their love for their country, *Dannebrog* now serves to remind the Danish people of their rich heritage and richly endowed land—a colorful country, where the smell of the fresh sea air, the sound of the village church bell, the echoes of victorious struggles of the past, as well as the ever-present tides of future challenge, stir patriots and visitors alike to sing in praise the national anthem, *Der er et yndigt land*—"There is a lovely land."

Here is the anthem as translated by S. D. Rødholm:

> There is a lovely land
> Where stand the shady beeches
> Near salty eastern strand
> With hills that gently rise and fall.
> Its name is dear old Denmark,
> And it is Freya's hall.
>
> There in the ancient days
> The armored Vikings rested
> Between their bloody frays.
> Then they went forth the foe to face
> And found in stone-set barrows
> Their final resting place.

This land is still as fair,
The sea as blue around it;
Now peace is cherished there.
Strong men and noble women still
Uphold old Denmark's honor
With faithfulness and skill.

Holger Danske (The Dane), the spirit of Denmark

CHAPTER 2

THE VIKING—THEN AND NOW

YOU MAY HAVE HEARD someone say, "He looks exactly like a Viking!" Immediately you picture a huge bearded blonde man, who has unusual vitality and is muscular and handsome in a rugged sort of way. Although the comment is perhaps meant to be flattering, a true Viking is not generally known as a pleasant or temperate individual.

Characteristic traits of the Vikings were their arrogance, their savage aggressiveness, their ruthless tactics in battle, and their fierce desire for power. Adventure and conquest were the Vikings' way of life. Regularly, they set out on marauding expeditions to far-off lands in their own well-crafted warships. In the height of their glory, they would return after their conquests, bringing back their plunder and boasting that they had attained the blessings of the gods, particularly Odin and Thor, and prepared themselves for the reward of Valhalla—the Viking heaven.

The meaning of the term *Viking,* or *vicingr,* is sometimes given as "sailor," with the connotation of "pirate" being attached later. Alternately, the word is sometimes interpreted as meaning "creek" or "bay," from which the Vikings presumably set sail on their adventuresome voyages. Generally, Vikings are identified with those early Scandinavians who raided and conquered distant coasts from about A.D. 789 to A.D. 1050.

Usually no distinction is made among the Scandinavian national groups in the earliest history of the Viking age. It is known that great numbers of Vikings came from Norway, Sweden, Finland, and Denmark, and that their expeditions affected the course of history in Scandinavia and in the lands they conquered. Historians do agree, however, that the Danes made separate and significant conquests apart from other Norsemen. From the year 789, when the first recorded Viking raid was made on the English coast, the Danes colonized countless islands and continued to attack the coast of Scotland and England off and on for more than two hundred years, settling there in great numbers. In fact, the English empire was for a time united under Danish rule, with Canute the Great serving as king from 1017 until his death in 1035. He reigned as king of Denmark at the same time.

The story is often told how King Canute tried to prove that he was divine by commanding the sea to halt before him. But when the tide continued to roll in over his feet, the exalted and proud Viking humbly had to admit to his mortal state.

The incident may be a legend, but it symbolizes a fitting transition of the Danes from Viking times to the Christian era, for later in his reign King Canute made a pilgrimage to Rome, confessed his sins, and changed his attitude completely, becoming a strong believer in and supporter of the church.

The Vikings made numerous excursions to other lands besides England, touching Iceland, Greenland, and North America, and leaving their mark in the wake of their marauding expeditions. Remnants of Scandinavian culture, customs, dialect, and names remain in some form in all these areas.

The Scottish word for church, *kirk,* is the same as the Danish *kirke,* and the similar words *baern* and *børn,* meaning children, show the presence of Danish settlers in Scotland. Places like Sandwich and Norwich in England bear the ending *wich,* or *vic,* (for Viking), as a result of Danish conquest there. Of wider consequence, the Viking excursions produced descendants of mixed ancestry, as the Danes brought home wives and mistresses to their native land or settled permanently on foreign soil.

The Vikings had many reasons for their reckless pursuits. First, it would seem that they engaged in dangerous ventures to prove themselves valiant and courageous. Upon returning from one of their many fierce voyages, they were warmly welcomed by their native people, who celebrated their return with exuberance, usually for days at a time. Women served horns filled with mead, and amid drinking and laughter the Vikings would play games of chance, using dice and counters. Sometimes they sent up burnt offerings to the gods, and always they sang of their forefathers' achievements, lustily drinking to even greater deeds in days to come.

A second reason was that every hardy Norseman was expected to engage in war. The customary weapons were battle-ax, sword, and bow. Wearing a conical helmet with nose cover and a coat of mail or leather garment, holding a shield before him, the warrior felt well protected. However, at times he would show his courageous nature by removing his shirt *(serk)* before a battle and, armed only with a club, engage his enemy in combat. The term *berserk,* meaning "without a shirt," stems from this demonstration.

The acquisition of additional fertile land was another important reason for the Viking raids; food supplies were needed by the settlements back in Denmark. The country was somewhat barren at that time, the soil was poor, and natural resources were scarce. As a result, farms were scattered and few. Most of the Danes settled in towns built around garrisons, where food could be brought in from overseas trading and raiding.

Four such garrison towns have been found in Denmark, the largest of which is Aggersborg, situated on Limfjorden near the present city of Ålborg on Jutland. Many of the raids on England began in Aggersborg because of its convenient location. The only Viking town to be completely excavated is Trelleborg on Zealand, where the remains reveal most clearly the nature of homes and the lifestyle of the Viking inhabitants.

Another reason the Danes wanted more land at this time was that they competed fiercely with other countries— especially Sweden and Norway—for status, which was symbolized in the acquisition of land.

Finally, it should be stressed that the Vikings were not raiders only; they were traders as well. It is often said that they came "with a scale in one hand and a sword in the other."

Many legendary tales from the Viking period have come down to us, revealing significant characteristics of these people. Denmark in earlier times was not one unified kingdom, but a cluster of kingdoms, each one under a separate ruler. The story is told of King Edmund of Jutland, who was deeply ashamed of his great hulk of a son, Uffe. Uffe was strong but careless and casual, apparently uninterested in wars. "My son will never use my good sword, Skrep, with honor," moaned the king, and he ordered it buried in the ground.

But when King Edmund was old and blind, the Saxon king sent word to Denmark that Edmund must either give up his kingdom or meet him on the battleground. Then, surprisingly, Uffe stepped forward to avenge that insult. "Tell your king that I will alone take on his son in battle, and not only him but the largest giant he wants to bring."

While King Edmund rejoiced but worried over this turn of events, Uffe hunted for armor big enough to fit him and had a special sword fashioned for the fight. "No," cried Uffe, "this sword will not do!" So the king ordered his own sword Skrep to be dug up and placed in Uffe's hand.

"Ah, this suits me better," laughed the huge prince, and he proceeded to swing Skrep about, cutting down everything he touched.

The contest took place on an island in the Ejder River, and many Danes and Germans lined the banks. Old King Edmund sat out on the river's edge, ready to drown himself if his son should go down in defeat. But Uffe easily slew both the Saxon prince and the giant he had brought with him. Once again Denmark's honor was saved. So was Prince Uffe's.

Within the National Museum in Copenhagen, many relics of the Viking age have been preserved, including those of exhumed Viking ships. One of the early ships discovered was in a burial mound in Ladby in northern Funen. There, in 1930, while plowing a field close to the fjord, farmer Erik Eriksen turned up bones belonging to Viking men and women. These seemed to have been poor folk, since they were buried without jewels or ornaments. Several years later, Eriksen turned up a coffin containing the body of a woman with a number of valuable jeweled bracelets.

These findings made Eriksen think that the earth mound adjacent to this burial ground might contain the bones of other, more noteworthy, personages. He made arrangements, therefore, to have this mound excavated under the direction

of an archeologist from the National Museum in Copenhagen. After six months of careful excavating, researchers
uncovered a seventy-two-foot Viking ship, buried with a
Viking chieftain. A carbon-dating process revealed the vessel
to be more than a thousand years old.

In the ship were found the bones of twelve horses which
had been sacrificed, as well as a number of dogs intended
to provide companionship for the chieftain's stay in Valhalla.
Hundreds of additional artifacts were found, most of which
are housed in the National Museum in Copenhagen.

The ship on Eriksen's farm was not moved, and a large
structure was built around it. Then the mound was rebuilt
over it, to its former dimensions. Today you can enter the
cave under the mound and view the preserved ship.

For five hundred years, the fishermen and navigators in
the town of Roskilde had known that a reef of underwater
rocks was obstructing the channel of the Roskilde Fjord
and preventing deep-draft ships from approaching the city.
According to one legend, the barrier was a medieval ship
sunk by Queen Margrethe I of Denmark in 1412 to guard
the entrance to the harbor and prevent enemy ships from
approaching the city of Roskilde, which was then the capital
of the combined kingdoms of Denmark, Norway, and
Sweden.

In 1926, a channel was dredged around the underwater
reef to enable large ocean vessels to approach the city's
harbor. Fragments of wood were brought out, and they were
found to be older than the supposed five hundred years.

In 1957, scuba divers found further evidence that the
boats were of the Viking age. Not one but several boats had
been sunk to guard the channel from the Norwegian Viking
marauders, who probably were attempting to sack the rich
trading center of Roskilde.

During the next two summers, divers obtained enough evidence to warrant the mounting of a full-scale expedition to recover as much of the treasure as possible. Six individual ships were discovered, ranging in size from a small ferry or fishing boat forty feet in length to a large longship (raiding warship) ninety feet in length.

Removing these Viking ships from the bottom of the fjord was a monumental task. More than fifty thousand parts first had to be placed into plastic sacks, later to be identified and assembled. In 1969, a modern museum was built in Roskilde for the reconstruction of these ships. Here the various vessels are on display, while workers are constantly busy at their intricate task of rebuilding them.

The Vikings' knowledge of ship design was amazing. The largest ship being reassembled in Roskilde is a *knarr*, an ocean-going cargo ship whose maker was evidently acquainted with the science of hydrodynamics. The beautifully streamlined underwater lines of this ship resemble those of a modern specialized yacht designed for speed. Viking ships also had only forty inches of freeboard under water, allowing them to land smoothly on the beach.

Scandinavians are credited with inventing the keel, a device that gave ships of this type stability and seaworthiness. The construction had to be sturdy to resist the pressure of the high ocean waves.

The Viking age ended at the close of the tenth century. Although it is interesting and intensely significant to the history of all Scandinavia, it was only a prelude to the ultimate direction that the Danish history would later take. The conquests of territories and the importation of foreign cultures did have some effect on the nature of developments, but Danes who had remained at home from the expeditions had cleared lands, improved agriculture, and established forms of government as well as estates.

Traces of the Viking from the distant past may still be visible in the character of the Danish people today. The love of discovery is clearly perceptible in their fervor for pursuing archeological studies. This trait is also evidenced in other fields of science—as well as in government, education, and the arts.

The vigor of the Viking still prevails in the strong physical constitution of Danish men and women today. One need only observe Danish preschool children on their daily walk through slush and snow, or bundled babies sleeping in their outdoor cradles in the wintertime, to realize that from an early age the Danes are routinely exposed to the elements to give them physical fitness.

Another identifiable Viking trait is the courage the Danes often show in the face of suffering and tragedy. With an impervious mask, they are able to hide inner feelings of pain. Such was the case during World War II, when Denmark was occupied by Nazi Germany. During this crisis, the nation's greatest asset was the spirit of its people.

This courage was exemplified by the dauntless valor of their king. One day, when the siren sounded for the clearing of the streets in wake of a threatened bombing of the city of Copenhagen, a lone rider on a fine horse was seen riding down the street, unafraid. It was King Christian X, boldly reassuring his people.

In the work of the "underground" during the same trying period, Danish patriots, outwardly calm and unperturbed, were secretly saving thousands of Danish Jews from capture by getting them across the border into Sweden, a neutral country.

Also during the Nazi occupation, the talented and versatile Piet Hein invented "grooks," short poems with cartoon drawings to help keep up public morale. They were also used to fool the Germans, who could not understand their double meaning. One of the grooks is appropriately entitled, "A Maxim for Vikings":

A MAXIM FOR VIKINGS

Here is a fact
   that should help you to fight
     a bit longer:

Things that don't act-
   ually kill you outright
     make you stronger.

The better character traits of the Viking seem to have survived in the Dane of today. However, these peace-loving and peace-living Scandinavians, who love their land and home, have few of the fiercer traits of the warring Nordic conquerors of the past. Some would even rather not hear you mention their distant relationship!

Hamlet's Castle at Elsinore

Chapter 3

KINGS AND QUEENS

How has the little kingdom of Denmark managed to survive a thousand years of strifeful history to become a peaceful, democratic monarchy of modern times? What indelible marks have the sovereigns through the ages left on the pages of Denmark's annals? What worthy legacies did the monarchs bequeath? For the history of Denmark *is* its monarchy: fifty-three kings and two queens, through their deeds or example, have endowed the land with either folly or fortune. Described in this chapter are some of the most significant influences and most colorful events.

The Vikings were busy conquering and colonizing distant shores when Gorm the Old became king (860-935) of the section of Denmark called Jutland. Gorm had two sons, Knud and Harald. Gorm loved Knud especially, and he swore to kill anyone who should bring him news of Knud's death. When Knud was killed in a Viking raid, the people were afraid to tell him. His wife found a way to impart the news, however. She brought to the king Knud's royal robes and added all the vestments used at funerals. Gorm got the message and exclaimed, "My son is dead!"

Thyra replied, "You said it, not I." Gorm himself died the next day of sorrow. He was buried in Jelling, the seat of government, where Thyra later was buried as well. Their son Harald erected a memorial stone, inscribed, "King

Harald erected this monument in memory of Gorm, his father, and Thyra, his mother, that same Harald who subdued all Denmark and Norway and converted the Danes to Christianity." This is the oldest runic stone to be seen in Denmark today.

In the year 1016, Gorm's great-grandson, Canute the Great—who became a devout Christian—conquered England and established his reign over that country as well as Denmark, Sweden, Norway, Iceland, and Greenland. Canute distinguished himself as one of the ablest administrators ever to come out of the north. While residing in England, this staunch supporter of the Christian church sent many bishops back to Denmark to spread Christianity throughout the country.

However, after the death of Canute I and the ascension of Edward the Confessor to the throne of England, the extensive kingdom over which Canute had ruled fell apart. A series of civil wars as well as wars among the various countries ensued for a hundred years until Valdemar the Great was acclaimed King of Denmark in 1137. He reunited the kingdom and also conquered the island of Rugen.

One of the wisest decisions of Valdemar the Great was to appoint his friend and foster brother, Absalon, as Archbishop of Lund. Absalon was not only a great archbishop, but he also was the founder of the city of Copenhagen. Today you may see his golden memorial statue prominently placed in front of the city hall in the city square.

Valdemar the Great was also the first to establish the policy of hereditary monarchy in Denmark. At his death in 1182, he was widely mourned for his success in attaining national and spiritual unity.

Expansion of territory continued under King Valdemar II, who reigned from 1202-1241. Hailed as Valdemar the Victorious *(Valdemar Sejr),* he conquered Pomerania, Estonia, and parts of Mecklenburg, and he became sovereign over all of Denmark, southern Sweden, and the entire Baltic coast.

According to legend, it was during the reign of Valdemar the Victorious that the Danish flag came into being at the height of the Battle of Lyndaniz against the Estonians, on June 15, 1219. The Danes were losing, until a red banner with a white cross is said to have been dropped from heaven. For the Danish crusaders, it was a miraculous symbol, and the tide of defeat was turned into one of victory. *Dannebrog* was adopted by the Danish army under Valdemar the Victorious and later became the Danish national flag.

All Danes are familiar with the story of the good and beautiful Queen Dagmar, the beloved wife of Valdemar the Victorious. King Valdemar had heard of the lovely daughter of the King of Bohemia and sought to marry her. His offer was accepted with pleasure, and Dagmar was escorted to Denmark aboard a barge with great ceremony. She was a magnificent queen, sweet and gentle in her ways, and her overwhelming kindness made all the people idolize her.

Among her requests was one for the release of a certain bishop and other captives from unjust imprisonment. But the king was afraid. "The boors are unworthy of freedom. They must be humbled. If they are once restored to freedom, they will rise up and kill me!"

Dagmar replied, "Heaven is my judge. If you, proud king, refuse to do these acts of simple justice, I shall not stay with you but shall return to my father's house." And she removed the crown from her head and handed it to the king, saying, "I give you back that which you brought to me."

King Valdemar looked at her with admiration, saying, "No, fair one, take back the crown. Nothing shall be denied you. Before the bell strikes one, my gallant knights shall ride to Attenborg and loose the captives' chains." The king kept his promise, and the knights released the prisoners.

Following his release, the grateful bishop came in person to thank the kind queen, who had also managed to abolish the tax of the poor. Bells rang, and people cried with joy, while children and peasants threw wild flowers in the path of the queen. Happiness flooded the land, and the name of Queen Dagmar was on everyone's lips.

But the joyous time was to last only seven years. Dagmar died in childbirth, and on her deathbed she begged the king not to take the wicked Portuguese princess, Berengard, for a wife. Unfortunately, Valdemar failed to keep his promise. Soon after Dagmar's death he married the cruel and false Berengard, who came to be hated as intensely as Dagmar was loved. Berengard's name came to stand for everything that was bad, and in Denmark it is still frequently used with that meaning.

The death of Valdemar the Victorious was followed by many years of civil war, resulting in disruption of the monarchy and governmental institutions. In fact, for eight years, 1332 to 1340, the country was without a monarch, until in 1340 Valdemar IV became king. Acclaimed as *Valdemar Atterdag* (*Atter dag* meaning "a new day") this king chose to use strategy instead of force to reunite the state and regain lost territory. And after twenty years of struggle he succeeded.

Known as the greatest Danish medieval king, Valdemar IV established a strong national army in which peasants and nobles shared equal rank. He built a chain of castles, the wardens of which became leaders of the local administration.

When Valdemar IV died in 1375, he left no direct male heirs. Oluf, his grandson, became the successor to the throne. But since he was only five years old, his mother, Margrethe, daughter of Valdemar and wife of King Haakon VI of Norway, reigned as regent. Haakon died in 1380, and then Norway also came under Margrethe's rule. When Oluf died seven years later, Margrethe was chosen as queen. Meanwhile, Sweden deposed its king, Albrecht of Mecklenburg, and the noblemen elected Margrethe as their sovereign ruler.

This story is told about Sweden's King Albrecht, who was related to the Danish royalty and made claims to both thrones. He had insulted Queen Margrethe by calling her "King Pantless" and by sending her emery stones to sharpen her needles, suggesting that she stick to sewing! Albrecht boasted he would not wear his "cap," or crown, before he had conquered both Denmark and Norway. But Swedish nobles favored Margrethe's rule and allowed her to send troops to Sweden to capture the king. After Margrethe's armies won the battle of Falkøping (1389), Albrecht was imprisoned for seven years. Margrethe punished him by making him wear a cap with a pointed tassel nine yards long!

In 1397, Margrethe's rule ended when Eric of Pomerania, her infant nephew and nearest of kin, became king of Norway and of Denmark and Sweden as well. However, Margrethe continued to rule as Eric's regent until her death in 1412. By the Union of Kalmar in 1397, these three countries —as well as Iceland, Greenland, the Faroe Islands, and parts of Finland—were all united into one kingdom, a union which was to last for 126 years. Sweden and a portion of Finland seceded in 1523; Norway declared her independence in 1814; and Iceland became independent in 1944. Greenland and the Faroes are still under Danish rule.

After Eric of Pomerania died, Christian I (1448-1481), of the House of Oldenborg, came to the throne. He began a long succession of Danish kings. Except for one king (Hans, 1481-1513) every king from Christian I through Frederik

IX was titled alternately either Christian or Frederik until 1972, when Queen Margrethe II ascended the throne, again interrupting the sequence.

Some familiar names date back to the time of Christian I, including the name Rosenkrantz. King Christian was to have an audience with the Pope in Rome and took with him, as an aide, Otto Nielsen of Herningsholm. The Pope presented a gold violet to the king and a crown of roses to Otto. When Otto was knighted, he adopted the name of Rosenkrantz as the family name in remembrance of the Pope's gift of roses. Shakespeare liked the name and used it, along with that of Guildenstern (for *Gyldenstjerne,* meaning "golden star") for Hamlet's friends.

Holger Rosenkrantz was sent as Danish ambassador to the government established by Oliver Cromwell in England. Cromwell scorned the young man because he wore no beard and did not hesitate to tell him so. Young Rosenkrantz answered, "If my sovereign had known it was a beard you required, he could have sent you a goat. At any rate, my beard is of older date than your protectorate."

During the reigns of Christian II, III, and IV, and of Frederik I, II, and III, from 1513 through 1670, one civil war followed another. Christian II (1513-1523), often called Christian the Cruel, was a friend of the lowly peasant, but very unpopular with the nobles, who held monopoly over lands and control over the peasants.

In 1520, after a period of unrest in Sweden, King Christian II, opposed by the nobility but supported by commoners, entered Stockholm to be crowned hereditary king of Sweden. He invited all the leading aristocrats to the coronation festivities, including eighty-two noblemen and political leaders, even though they were his enemies. Then, at the height of the celebration, he had them all seized and in a rigged trial saw that they were condemned and beheaded on the spot.

This despotic act became known as the Blood Bath of Stockholm, and it was followed by even more persecutions. Finally, a young Swedish noble, Gustav Vasa, whose father had been one of the Blood Bath victims, led a rebellion that resulted in Christian's dethronement and his escape to The Netherlands. With the help of the common people, who still supported him, Christian attempted several times to restore himself to the throne. But he was finally imprisoned for life under Frederik II. He lies buried in Saint Canute's Cathedral in Odense. A portrait of his first wife, Elisabeth, whom he married when she was only thirteen and who died at age twenty-five, is carved on the altar piece.

Christian IV (1588-1648), called "the Builder King," reigned impressively over Denmark for a period of sixty years. Since he was only eleven years old when his father, Frederik II, died, a regency of four members of the *Rigsdag* (the parliament) ruled for him for a short time. But soon after his coronation it was apparent he would become one of Denmark's greatest kings. He equipped a better navy and army, established trading companies, and sent out expeditions as far as Greenland. He encouraged artistic endeavors by inviting foreign painters, masterbuilders, weavers, and craftsmen to Denmark. Bringing in Dutch architects and engineers, he laid out many new cities not only in Denmark, but in Norway as well. Numerous public buildings and several score of the country's finest palaces and churches are credited to Christian IV. In the city of Copenhagen alone, this masterbuilder's hand left ingenious examples of its skill. It is said that he worked with his own hands on the dragon's tail spire of *Børsen,* the stock exchange.

King Christian IV was also called "the Sailor King," since

he was interested in the design and construction of ships of all kinds and was always concerned with the welfare of the sailors. It is not surprising, therefore, that he had rows of neat and cozy houses built for sailors near the harbor. These charming houses, called *Nyboder,* are now reserved for pensioned sailors of the Royal Danish Navy.

One of Denmark's national songs, *Kong Kristian Stod ved Højen Mast* [King Christian stood at the main mast], is based on the following incident during the reign of Christian IV: When trouble arose between Sweden and Denmark, the old king, in spite of lack of support from the parliament, called out his troops. He himself commanded his ship, *Trefoldigheden,* and was already wounded when a cannon-ball splintered the vessel. He was thought dead, but as the enemy sought to pull down the flag, he shouted, "No, God has given me strength and courage to strive for my people as long as each person does his duty." He did survive and fought on to victory in that battle. But the war itself was lost, and Sweden gained many privileges and much land, plus toll-free passage through the straits.

Honored as one of Denmark's most revered kings, *Kong Kristian* died at the age of seventy-one and lies buried in Roskilde Cathedral, the Westminster Abbey of Denmark. All except three of the kings and four of the queens since Christian I, along with the sovereign ruler Queen Margrethe I, are entombed in this magnificent cathedral, the finest in Denmark.

The next four kings in succession, known along with Christian IV as "Builder Kings," erected imposing monuments of architectural note.

Christian V (1670-1699), the third "Builder King," planned a great many castles, but only a few of them were actually constructed. However, it was during this time, about

1690, that Clausholm Castle, located near Ålborg in Jutland, was built for Count Reventlow, the king's chancellor. Here, Anna Sophie, the daughter of Count Reventlow, was born. King Frederik IV (1699-1730) eloped with the nineteen-year-old Anna Sophie in 1712 while still married to Queen Louise, but he married her legally when Louise died nine years later. Upon King Frederik's death in 1730, Anna Sophie, called "the Conscience Queen," was banished from the court by Christian VI, son of Frederick IV and Queen Louise. She was taken to Clausholm Castle, where she remained until her death in 1743. Her crown and coat of arms were painted on the wooden doors at the entrance and may still be seen there.

Frederik IV, the fourth of the "Builder Kings," is responsible for the lovely swan-white Fredensborg Palace, which lies on the road between Frederiksborg and Elsinore in northern Zealand. He also instigated a number of reforms, including the formation of a local militia, abolition of serfdom, and the founding of 240 elementary schools throughout Denmark.

An account of this period of Danish history would not be complete without reference to the naval hero Tordenskjold. Stories about him are repeated in story and song by all Danes. Born Peder Vessel in Trondhjem, this national hero worked himself up from a lowly seaman to a captain of a ship with thirty cannons. Having led Denmark to many victories in its sea battles against Sweden, he was acclaimed by King Frederik IV: "For your loyalty, courage, and enthusiasm you have been advanced in rank. You shall henceforth be called Tordenskjold [thunder warrior]."

"Tordenskjold!" exclaimed Peder Vessel happily. "Now I shall really thunder in the ears of the Swedes, so that all may know you did not give me this name in vain." And thunder he did. The stories of his exploits are legion.

Under the last "Builder King," Christian VI (1730-1746), Renaissance enlightenment began to influence the activities of the government. This king, who is said to have had no mistresses and waged no wars, encouraged the pursuit of scientific studies, built costly buildings, and maintained a magnificent court. But he also placed the country under puritanical rule, instituting compulsory church attendance and banning such pleasures as stage productions, dancing, and celebrations.

According to the dramatist Ludwig Holberg, the reign of Frederik V (1746-1766) was "one of bliss," when everything seemed to gain new life and energy. Unlike Christian VI, this king enjoyed fun and joyful living and changed the tone at the court from one of solemnity to one of gaiety. He ordered the strict rules relaxed and infused a new spirit into daily living, thus establishing himself as one of the most popular of Danish kings.

This monarch was interested in art and education, and he ordered the establishment of academies for artists, sculptors, painters, and architects. Frederik V also opened a foster home for poor boys and built Frederik's Hospital. Beautiful new streets were laid out at his command, and Amalienborg Square and Castle had their beginning under his rule.

Amalienborg Square is the finest memorial of all those that King Frederik V left behind. In the years between 1750 and 1760, the king allowed four noblemen to build palaces to enclose the octagonal square, on the condition that they all engage the same architect, Nicolai Eigtved, and adhere to the same style, namely baroque design. In the center of the square was placed an equestrian statue of Frederik himself.

The arrangement of the buildings in the square is uniquely

effective. The harbor and masts and rigging of passing ships can be seen between two palaces in one direction, and the Marble Church, with its gleaming copper dome resembling St. Peter's in Rome, can be seen between the two opposite palaces. The structures are probably some of the finest examples of rococo architecture in Europe.

Christian VII, who succeeded Frederik V, moved into Amalienborg after fire destroyed the Christiansborg Castle in 1794. The Crown purchased all four palaces to house the king and his family, and since that time Amalienborg has been the official residence of Danish sovereigns.

When Frederik VI became king in 1808, he was faced with problems from within and without the country. The year before he ascended the throne, England had demanded that he surrender his fleet to help the British ward off Napoleon's threatened invasion. When Denmark refused, the British bombarded Copenhagen and forced the Danes to surrender the fleet. To prevent a British invasion, the Danes concluded an alliance with Napoleon. Sweden allied itself with Britain and Russia against France and Denmark, and when Napoleon was defeated in 1814, Norway was ceded to Sweden at the Peace Treaty of Kiel. This final loss cut the boundaries of Denmark to approximately its present area.

As Prince Regent, Frederik VI had been responsible for major reforms, such as freeing the serfs, abolishing the *Stavsbaand* law, which had tied the peasants to the landed estates, and promoting trade and education. His royal dignity, his kindness, and his concern for the people endeared him to the Danes. He has been called "the father of the country" because of his energetic, responsible, and upright conduct of Denmark's affairs during trying times.

A most important step in the political progress of Den-

mark was taken when King Frederik VII (1848-1863) re-
nounced absolute monarchy and signed a new constitution,
Grundloven, on June 5, 1849. A constitutional monarchy
was instituted—the type of government now existing in Denmark. *Rigsdag* (the parliament), was to be composed of
two houses, the *Landsting* (representing the landowners and
nobles), and the *Folketing* (representing the common people). It was the first representative government in the land
for one hundred and fifty years. The constitution also
granted more freedoms—freedom of speech, religion, and
personal liberty.

When Frederik VII died, his son Christian IX (1863-
1906) came to the throne. This king became the father-in-
law of many of the crowned heads of Europe. He had ten
children, to whom he was devoted, and for whom he succeeded in providing advantageous marriages throughout
Europe, as dukes, duchesses, queens, kings, and empresses.
Because of his preoccupation with maintaining family status,
King Christian's political and social gains were not great.

Christian X (1912-1947) has been called "the War
King" because his reign spanned two of the most horrible
holocausts of modern times. He came to the throne two
years before the outbreak of World War I and guided Denmark in a policy of neutrality through this conflict. Rising
prices and inflation forced government controls and the
beginning of a regulated economy, which has evolved into
the present social welfare state.

Ten months after Germany and Denmark had signed
their ten-year nonaggression pact in 1939, eighty thousand
Nazi troops moved across the border of southern Jutland
on April 9, 1940. From hiding places in Copenhagen,
thousands of Germans emerged to take over strategic points.
Armed soldiers approached the Royal Guards in Amalien-

borg Square, who, loyal to their king to the last, fired on the approaching enemy and in so doing lost their lives. Then Denmark was to feel the sting of World War II.

At 6:30 A.M., two hours after the invasion on that fateful day, King Christian decided to capitulate. It was a black hour for Denmark. For five years during the occupation, the Germans tried to subdue Denmark politically and socially— even physically. For a time, the Danish king and the government were allowed to function. News media carried on as usual, and elections were permitted. But in August 1943, when the king and parliament rejected the Nazi demand that a state of emergency be declared, the German commander himself proclaimed a state of emergency and enforced martial law. Executive power had been taken over by the Germans. Immediately, the Danish vice-admiral gave an order for the Danes to scuttle their ships in the harbor. In reprisal, the Germans confined the king to Sorgenfri Palace at Lyngby near the Frilandsmuseet.

Sorgenfri (meaning "carefree") had been built in 1705 and enlarged in 1735 as a residence for Frederik V when he was Crown Prince. Now it became a famous place of confinement. While imprisoned by the Nazis, King Christian was shot at through a window by an unknown assailant. The pane of glass with the hole in it has been preserved and is on display.

The Germans were intent on seeking out Jews and sending them to concentration camps. But the Danish resistance movement became so well organized that out of seventy-seven hundred Jews in Denmark, all but five hundred managed to escape the Nazis. Government leaders, ministers, and doctors had gone into hiding and were working underground. One group called itself The Sewing Circle and managed to smuggle hundreds of Jews across the Kattegat from Jutland into Sweden—the scientist Niels Bohr among them—before the Nazis tightened controls and placed further restrictions on the activities of the people. When the German commander imposed an 8:00 P.M. curfew, the Danes, who enjoyed the long evening daylight hours, showed their displeasure. Strikes were called and the Danes left their jobs during the day to be able to work their vegetable gardens before eight o'clock. The Germans became provoked and turned off the water and electricity, but the Danes were resourceful. They cooked over open fires and carried water from nearby lakes.

Despite cruelty and terror, the Danes were able to hold firm, using their ingenious tactics of self-preservation, and they survived. On May 5, 1945, when news came that the Allied forces had broken through and that the Germans had capitulated, a jubilant people laughed and wept for joy.

A song which was later to become the new "flag song" for Denmark was written by one of the strongest resisters in World War II, Poul Sørensen, and sung for the first time in a little cabaret in Copenhagen in November 1940. Later it was published in magazines and newspapers and broadcast over the radio. The Germans finally realized that the song contained dangerous overtones, but too late, for the words had already taken hold and given the Danes a renewed spirit of strength.

The last stanza is:

> Det Flag, der blaeser i Danmark
> det har Modgangens Storm foldet ud.
> Dets Farver var aldrig saa rene som nu
> mod Uvejrets drivende Slud.
> Lidt slapt og lidt udvisket blev det
> i Solskin—men nu kan vi se det!
> Nu smaelder det kraftigt og haardt.

Et Flag er smukkest i Modvind,
Saa føler vi først, det er vort.

Translated, it reads:

This flag that waves in Denmark
has struggle's storm unfolded;
Its colors were never as clear as now
against the whirlwind's driving dust.
Faded and slackened it became
in the sun. But now we can see it,
restored, unshattered and sound!
A flag is loveliest in the storm,
when we realize at last it is ours!

Their sense of humor was another weapon the Danes had against the invaders, and they used it to best advantage. Piet Hein's "grooks" have already been mentioned, and other examples of humor abound. During this frightening time, a well-known Danish actress read over the Danish radio, in a program of national poems, one entitled "Vort Modersmaal":

De Fremmede, de taenkte at volde hende Sorg;
de bød hende Traeldom i hendes egen Borg;
Men just som de mente, hun var i Baand og Bast,
da lo hun saa hjertelig, at alle Laenker brast.

Strangers thought they could cause her deepest sorrow.
They offered her slavery in her own land.
But just as they thought they had her tied and chained,
She laughed so heartily that the links gave way.

After the war, a new coalition government of party representatives and resistance leaders was set up to make an effective transition to peacetime conditions. Old political parties resumed their former strength. But the postwar years were difficult ones. Restrictions had to be made to save the economy and maintain exchange rates. As industry began to recuperate and foreign trade was resumed, the nation began to stabilize.

During his reign, Christian X had extended the franchise to women in 1915, given Iceland its independence in 1944, lowered the voting age from thirty-five to twenty-five, and abolished special votes for the privileged. He became a national symbol of Danish solidarity and was much beloved and respected as a great national leader.

King Frederik IX, like his father, Christian, was a people's king. In as democratic a country as Denmark, a king's popularity is presumably based upon the interest he shows in his country. Frederik IX not only concerned himself with rights of the state, but also with the rights of the individual. Both he and his lovely wife, Queen Ingrid, and their daughters Margrethe, Benedikte, and Anne-Marie, mingled informally and warmly with the Danish people. The royal family, for Denmark, had become *real* as well as *regal*.

Of historic significance during King Frederik's reign was the signing of the new constitution on June 5, 1953, which abolished the *Landsting* and introduced a single chamber parliament, the *Folketing*. Also, it provided for female succession to the throne, which had been illegal since 1849. Not only was this clause consistent with Denmark's policy of equality, but it also anticipated the day when Princess Margrethe, the king's eldest daughter, should ascend the throne as next in line.

The appointment of an ombudsman, based on the Swedish model, and the lowering of the voting age to twenty-three were other constitutional provisions passed. In addition, Greenland came under Danish law and was given the right to send two members to the *Folketing*.

Frederik IX was buried in Roskilde Cathedral on January 24, 1972. A procession of royalty from all parts of Europe paid homage to the king.

The banner-covered casket of His Majesty King Frederik IX of Denmark, of the Wends and Goths, Duke of Slesvig, Holstein, Stormarn, Ditmarsken, Lauenborg, and Oldenborg was laid to rest beside the many monarchs who had left a pageantry of change and progress upon the realm of Denmark. The national anthem was played in final farewell.

But the kings and queens of Denmark do not die; they live in the many monuments they have left, in the hearts of the people, and in the songs written in loving tribute to their dedicated reigns. Here is Henry Wadsworth Longfellow's translation of *"Kong Kristian Stod ved Højen Mast,"* Denmark's royal anthem:

> King Christian stood by the lofty mast
> in mist and smoke;
> His sword was hammering so fast,
> through Gothic helf and brain it passed
> Then sank each hostile helm and mast,
> in mist and smoke.
> "Fly!" shouted they; "Fly, he who can,
> who braves of Denmark's Christian
> the stroke?"
>
> Path of the Dane to fame and might!
> Dark rolling wave!
> Receive thy friend who, scorning flight,
> Goes to meet danger with despite—
> Proudly as thou the tempest's might,
> Dark rolling wave!
> And amid pleasure and alarms,
> And war and victory, be thine arms
> My grave!

Fredensborg Castle
Inserts: Queen Margrethe and Prince Henrik

CHAPTER 4

THE REIGN OF A BELOVED QUEEN

"KING FREDERIK IX IS DEAD. Long live Her Majesty, Queen Margrethe II!" Three times the announcement rang out, according to custom, from the balcony of Christiansborg Palace in Copenhagen as Prime Minister Jens Otto Krag made the historic announcement. On January 17, 1972, Princess Margrethe, thirty-two-year-old daughter of King Frederik IX, was proclaimed Queen of Denmark, becoming the second woman ever to reign over that kingdom.

Margrethe's first act was to discard all other titles to which she could lay claim, stating she wished to be known simply as Queen Margrethe II, thereby relinquishing the previous titles: of the Wends and Goths, Duke of Slesvig, Holstein, Stormarn, Ditmarsken, Lauenborg, and Oldenborg. Accordingly, the traditional coat of arms was not suitable, and it became necessary for the queen to create a new royal arms, one which did not have all the symbols for these historical titles. The new arms bears at its center the cross of the national flag, *Dannebrog*.

The new monarch is also titled Countess Monpezat by her marriage in 1967 to handsome Count Henrik of France, renamed Prince Henrik of Denmark, and is mother of two young sons, Crown Prince Frederik and Prince Joachim. She has assumed her role as head of state of Denmark's constitutional monarchy through a long line of distinguished

ancestors, for although she did not take the long title of her
father, she is a direct descendant of the House of Oldenborg.

By royal custom, the young monarch has a long given
name—Margrethe Alexandrine Torhildur Ingrid. Alexandrine is for her grandmother, queen of King Christian X,
and Ingrid is for her mother, Queen Ingrid, wife of King
Frederik IX. The name Torhildur, a Faroese name, is
thought to have been given her because it represented the
part of Denmark that had not been occupied by the Germans
during World War II. Margrethe was born shortly after the
Germans took over Denmark in 1940.

With the name Margrethe, she is the first ruler not to
bear the traditional and familiar name of either Frederik or
Christian in alternate succession since the time of Christian
I, with the exception of Hans (1481-1513).

Frederik IX had no sons to inherit the throne. When, at
the age of thirteen, Margrethe accidentally found a newspaper story revealing that according to the new constitution
she would be heiress to the throne, she promptly burst into
tears. But after realizing the dimensions of the role she would
assume, she firmly decided she would be prepared for that
awesome day.

Margrethe attended Danish and English lower schools,
the Universities of Copenhagen and Århus, Cambridge University, London School of Economics, and the Sorbonne in
France. She is an avid reader, she loves to travel, and she
has a wide knowledge of both art and archeology. She is
fascinated by the latter and has traveled on many archeological expeditions. She even took part in the exhuming of artifacts from the Viking ships in the Roskilde Fjord in the
1960s. In 1975 she traveled to Leningrad, Moscow, and
other Russian cities. She was the first European monarch
to pay an official visit to the Soviet Union, and in 1976 she

visited the United States to honor its bicentennial.

In her girlhood, as Princess Margrethe, the queen had the opportunity and the freedom to grow up in a normal way, associating with other Danes and attending state schools. She and her two sisters, part of the close-knit royal family, became widely separated upon their marriages. Benedikte married Prince Richard of Sayn-Wittgenstein Berleburg, and Anne-Marie married King Constantine II of Greece. The natural, unsophisticated ways of the crown princess as a child are shown in many stories, such as the following: One day in school Margrethe was asked by a little friend whether she was happy that her father was king. "No," she answered, "but I am awfully happy that he is my father." When, after the marriage of both of her younger sisters, she was asked, "When are you going to find a husband?" the quick-witted princess replied, "He will have to find me!"

Even though Denmark is moving toward becoming a republic, general agreement prevails among the people that there is no point in creating a republic as long as Margrethe is on the Danish throne. The Danes are often heard to say, "We give our monarchs unlimited power, provided they don't use any of it." Actually, Margrethe's power is limited to signing laws already passed by the *Folketing*. As long as the monarchy is as democratic as it is and possesses the image of a people's government, this favorite symbol of Danish rule will remain.

It's interesting to compare the characters of the two Danish queens—Margrethe I and Margrethe II. The first Queen Margrethe, under whose rule Denmark, Norway, and Sweden became a united kingdom, had several characteristics similar to those of the present queen. She was intelligent; she was courageous; and she was gifted with a delightful Danish sense of humor. (Remember the nine-foot tassel she gave her royal prisoner?) As to status, both queens reigned over a highly respected monarchy.

In other respects, the two monarchs show opposing roles and contrasting natures. Margrethe I was "sovereign lady and ruler," who reigned supreme over the largest realm in Denmark's history. The advisory council had become insignificant in its influence, and the queen showed considerable partiality in appointing her own countrymen to the high offices in government. Ambitious and clever, she seized all property and estates for the crown, with an eye toward all possible territorial expansion.

By comparison, Queen Margrethe II rules over the smallest kingdom in Scandinavia. She works *with* the parliament in the enactment of laws, making those laws legal by affixing her signature. Conquest of land is out of the question, for the queen cannot use military force against foreign states except for the purpose of defense against armed attacks, unless by consent of the *Folketing*. Nor is she permitted to reign in other countries, except by the same parliamentary approval. According to the constitution, she must be a member of the Evangelical Lutheran Church, the established church of Denmark.

Denmark's constitution for two hundred years, from 1665 to 1849—called *Kongeloven*—granted the king unlimited powers. The new constitution of 1849—*Juni Grundloven* (the June Constitution)—was one of the most democratic constitutions of Europe. Thus the role of the king emerged from the most unlimited to the most limited monarchy in Christendom, and the government moved from extreme absolutism to parliamentary democracy. Of all the absolute monarchies in Europe, Denmark was the last to relinquish that title and become in name, as it had long been in practice, a constitutional monarchy.

Most of the provisions of the 1849 constitution are still in force, but the document has been revised four times, most recently on June 5, 1953. At that time, it was also established that the throne should be inherited by the descendants of King Christian X and Queen Alexandrine, either male or female, but that a son should take precedence over a daughter. If the monarch leaves no heir, the throne passes to his (or her) brother or sister (brother taking precedence), or to descendants "according to lineal descent."

It is interesting to note that "in order to maintain the constitution of the realm inviolably," the Queen Mother Ingrid enjoys regency rights which she may exert in case the present queen is incapacitated or out of the country. She is the first non-heir to enjoy this right.

Although executive power is vested in the reigning monarch, it is carried out through the ministers who are the heads of their respective ministries. The ministers, usually numbering eighteen besides the prime minister, meet in the Council of State *(Statsrådet)* under the presidency of the monarch to discuss political issues, new bills, and important international concerns.

The ministers have a political responsibility to the *Folketing,* for they draft the bills that are presented for consideration and debate in the parliament. If accepted, the bills are returned to the Council of State for the royal signature and counter signatures of one or more of the ministers.

Members of the *Folketing* are elected by a general vote of the people for a period of four years. The number of seats in parliament at the present time is 179, including two from Greenland and two from the Faroe Islands. Since 1961 the legal voting age has been twenty-one years, although factions in the government are recommending lowering the age to twenty or even eighteen.

Theoretically, the queen appoints the prime minister and the ministers. But the constitution of 1953 declares that the *Folketing* may pass a vote of censure on the prime minister and express a feeling of "no confidence" if a majority of the members oppose his or her views. The prime minister must then resign from the government, and a new election is ordered. Or, while serving as leader of the minority party, the prime minister may request the monarch to order a new election.

The largest single party in the *Folketing* from 1925 to 1972 was the Social Democratic Party, which advocates, according to its charter, "democratic socialism to promote human freedom, social security, and opportunity for individual development subject to social responsibility." In the December 1973 election it became a minority party for the first time. Since the party is supported by organized middle-class wage earners, small farmers, teachers, and civil employees, the effect of that loss of leadership is far-reaching.

A long-term leader of that party was Jens Otto Krag. In 1947, when only thirty-three years old, Krag became a member of the *Folketing* and also the minister of trade. In 1968 he was selected to head the Social Democratic majority party as prime minister. In 1972, immediately after Denmark's affiliation with the Common Market in Europe, Krag resigned "for personal reasons" after serving twenty-five years as a member of parliament.

Anker Jørgensen, who had been a member of *Folketing* for eight years and chairman of the country's largest labor union for four years, was selected to fill the leadership post. He was the first unskilled worker ever to be named prime minister. He held that position only until the 1973 election, when a man by the name of Poul Hartling, a member of the Venstre (Liberal Democrat) Party and Minister of Foreign

Affairs, was chosen to lead the country. After the national election of 1975, Anker Jørgensen was again chosen as Prime Minister, heading the Social Democratic party, now a minority party.

At the local level of government, important changes took place on April 1, 1970. At that time boroughs were abolished, and now the various areas of the nation are divided into county and town (or city) governmental units—*amtscommuner* and *primaecommuner,* respectively. Counties are governed by a county council, and a chairman is appointed by the central government for maintenance of roads, health, and hospital services. Under the new ruling, the local government, governed by an elected mayor and a city council, has more independent control over community development and greater financial means for industrial growth.

The women's liberation movement is rapidly being recognized in Denmark. Not only does Denmark have a woman as its reigning monarch, but women have also established a place for themselves in the parliament, in the *Statsråd* (Council of State), and in local governments.

In 1908 women were first permitted to hold office in the community government, but only 1.8 percent held such offices. Today there is protest among the female sex that they are being discriminated against, with only 10 percent of local and community government positions filled by women, except in Copenhagen and environs. For comparison, Danes cite Oslo, Norway, where more women than men have been elected to head the local governments.

A number of women have served and are serving in governmental posts. One of the new members of the *Folketing* in 1972 was a seventy-year-old woman, whom the joking Danes called the "great-grandmother of parliament." The youngest person ever to serve on the Danish cabinet was Tove

Nielsen, who was appointed by Prime Minister Hartling in 1972. A former schoolteacher, she was only thirty-two years old when she took office as Minister of Education. As a member of the *Venstre* Party, Tove Nielsen was brought up in politics and wrote her university thesis on the history of the political parties in Denmark. She had previously held the office of chief administrator of the Viborg community.

In 1974, of the twelve members appointed to the Committee on Culture headed by the Minister of Culture, eight were women and four were men. But here, also, the women claimed that prejudice was shown. The women affirm they are more often chosen to head committees on culture than committees on economy!

Truthfully, the Danes possess a deep respect for the rights of every individual. If this had not been true, the country might never have become a model of democratic socialism. However, every Danish citizen takes a keen interest in politics of government as well as in the problems of the individual. Perhaps the restlessness of the Viking still stirs in Danish blood, making the spirit of adventure clash with the automatic comforts provided by an all-inclusive welfare system. Perhaps the creative nature of the modern Dane is being challenged to develop a more coordinated and more enduring political program.

To her loyal subjects, Queen Margrethe represents a kingdom of integrity, dignity, and honor—a country to whose flag and customs they unfailingly pay their homage and respect.

Just before noon—day after day, year after year—from under the colonnade of Amalienborg Square in Copenhagen, thirty-six handsome young men, dressed in sky-blue trousers, red coats, and bearskin busbies, march snappily into the courtyard for the ceremonial changing of the royal guard.

In a colorful procession behind a thirty-one-piece band, the guards parade from the royal barracks to Amalienborg, weaving in and out of the streets for the benefit of spectators. Like toy soldiers from Andersen's fairy tales, these serious-looking, loyal guards take over their faithful watch of the home of their beloved ruler and royal family. As the red-and-white *Dannebrog* is set in place and the band begins its noon concert, the significance of this spot becomes real.

Amalienborg is a meaningful monument, not only to all the noble sovereigns who have dwelt within its walls, but also to a young queen who, bearing the weight of a country's problems on her shoulders, still reigns over a democratic nation in which the voice of the people is heard emphatically in the resolution of critical issues of the times.

Long live Queen Margrethe II!

The five swans, symbol of Nordic unity

CHAPTER 5

WORLD CONSCIOUSNESS

IN SPITE OF DENMARK'S small land area, it exerts as much
influence in the political and social affairs of the world today
as some of the largest countries. Denmark has a world out-
look that encompasses not only the free democratic societies
but the entire Third World as well. Danish foreign policy
may be summed up in these words: "Help live and let live."
For the Danes not only love life and freedom, they also love
people. Being one of the most tolerant as well as efficient of
nations, Denmark views other countries with consideration,
and it attempts—within the limits of its resources and skill—
to help those who need and ask for assistance.

This enlightened foreign policy is supported by the Ministry of Foreign Affairs, through which Denmark is represented
in fifty-three embassies around the world. Fifteen hundred
persons are employed on the foreign service staff—five hundred of whom are consulates, consulates general, and vice-
consulates in other countries. This ministry not only con-
ducts diplomatic relations between Denmark and other
nations, but it also governs matters pertaining to international law, trade relations, and treaties. Furthermore, it is
the official organ for the state's function in the United
Nations, the North Atlantic Treaty Organization, and other
international groups.

Denmark is in a position in which a strategic foreign policy is definitely to its best interests. The reasons for such a policy are clear: Denmark's geographic location at the open passages to the Baltic Sea places it in the line of world trade and makes it extremely vulnerable to attack. Its need for raw materials and for natural resources, especially energy, ranks Denmark as the largest export-import center, per capita, of any nation in the world. Denmark's proximity to the other Scandinavian countries and to the rest of Europe has made it particularly sensitive to world economic conditions.

The three Scandinavian countries of Denmark, Norway, and Sweden are bound together geographically, historically, and culturally by common ties. But cooperation among these countries does not mean a loss of national identity. Each nation has developed its own pattern for defending itself and for solving its internal economic problems. An effort was made in 1949 to form a coordinated Scandinavian defense council, but the attempt proved fruitless; and a plan for a Scandinavian common market in 1958 and 1959 was also unsuccessful. However, through persistent attempts to organize an effective, united body, the Nordic countries managed to establish, in 1952, the Nordic Council, composed of representatives from Denmark, Norway, Sweden, Iceland, and Finland. This group meets regularly to discuss common problems.

In spite of the fact that the power of the Nordic Council is limited to making recommendations to its respective governments, the council has succeeded in achieving closer practical connections among the five countries. Perhaps the most important result has been an expansion of trade, which grew nearly 220 percent between 1958 and 1969—Denmark's exports being the largest. Another accomplishment for the Nordic Council has been closer collaboration among the nations' firms, industrial organizations, cooperative societies, and professional organizations—all contributing to more efficient purchasing and marketing and to better exchange of information. A Swedish postage stamp, showing five graceful swans flying together, symbolizes the unified policy of the five countries.

An example of how communications benefited from this collaboration was the agreement of the national airways of each country to form the combined Scandinavian Airlines System—which is now one of the largest flight systems in the world.

But Denmark actually considers all countries its neighbors, since its relationship with one country virtually affects that with another. Consequently, Denmark strives to develop and maintain a policy of cooperation through its membership in European and world federations. For instance, the Council of Europe, in which Denmark is represented, promotes cooperation among European countries by supporting democratic government and by encouraging cultural exchanges.

While the European Free Trade Association (EFTA) has been of mutual advantage to all of its members, Denmark's contribution has been especially supportive. Its exports are greater to the countries of this association than to those in the European Economic Community (EEC, the Common Market).

Sweden receives most of Denmark's industrial exports, whereas Great Britain is still the recipient of most of its bacon and butter. Denmark would like, however, to see the cooperation expanded, especially in agricultural and industrial policy, so that its economic gain might be extended to the greater European market as well.

As a member of the United Nations and NATO, Denmark demonstrates in a fundamental and practical way its policy for world peace. Danish troops have been among many of the UN forces for keeping peace in the Middle East and have served for a number of years in Gaza—as well as in Cyprus and on the Suez Canal. Denmark also maintains a permanent emergency force to be called up at any time for the UN. Half of the Danish foreign allocations go to the Agency for International Development of the United Nations and to other international organizations. And 60 percent of the monetary budget of the foreign affairs ministry is devoted to relief and technical aid to developing nations as well as to the promotion of international cooperation.

During the Korean War, Denmark sent the hospital ship *Jutlandia* to Korea, as its contribution to the United Nations effort to preserve peace. A total of sixteen physicians, forty nurses, and twenty-five medical aid men, besides cooks, stewards, crew, and the world's most noted brain surgeon, Professor Edward Busch, made up the force of this famous hospital ship.

The Danes show a deep concern for the development and welfare of the emerging nations of Africa and Asia. Perhaps the very fact that Denmark is a land of security has led its government to stress the importance of assisting the less fortunate countries. To help provide a better life for these peoples, Denmark sends 1 percent of its gross national product to the developing countries and establishes medical missions throughout the Third World to vaccinate against contagious diseases. Other technical missions are sent to these countries to demonstrate dairy farming, hog raising, boat building, fishing, and many other skills.

For many years, the Danes have had an influence in foreign lands. As early as 1755, Danish traders colonized the small district in southern India called Frederiksnagore, named for Frederik V, as a basis for trading activities. This settlement remained under Danish rule only until 1845, but remnants of the Danish colonization still remain. The governor, Ole Bie, who was so industrious he was called by the British "the Beehive," built Saint Olaf's Church, where a Danish flag and Danish Bible remain in the sanctuary. Here in 1821 Serampore College was granted a royal charter by King Frederik VI, a charter which still is in effect.

In 1961, Denmark applied for full membership in the Common Market, conditional on only one requirement—that Great Britain, its best customer, would be admitted also. The negotiations broke down, and another attempt was made in 1967, but it was not until 1971 that a referendum was actually put to the people. Then, with a 64 percent majority, the Danes approved their country's participation in the EEC.

Denmark's hesitation in joining the Common Market was partly due to the feeling that "things could be worse." And so they could have been. For one thing, the Danes feared that the country might be overrun by other Europeans who would buy up all the summer houses or land set aside for leisure-time homes. There was also the consideration that the entry into the European Economic Community might affect the cooperative association that the Scandinavian countries had developed and expanded for themselves. This fear was allayed, however, when the Nordic Council countries concluded that Scandinavian cooperation could continue and might even be an asset should any one country decide to join the Common Market—at least as long as policies and procedures of each organization did not strikingly conflict.

The Danish farmers have had no reason to regret their support of Denmark's entry into the Common Market. The average income from Danish agriculture was almost doubled in the first year after entry, with an increase of 70 percent in farm exports. It is hoped that the removal of tariffs will eliminate trade barriers and stimulate manufacturing for the expanded market.

To counterbalance these benefits, however, there has been an increase of 6 percent in Danish food prices plus an expense of 5 million kroner, close to 1 million dollars, to pay for the new staff required to implement the EEC membership. These economic factors contribute to inflation and to the spiraling of costs and taxes, much to the dissatisfaction of restive Danes who are already afflicted by high taxes.

The long-term influences of Denmark's part in the EEC are yet to be seen. If the country can work out its internal economic interests satisfactorily, it is probable that membership in the larger European market may also effect a broader and stronger relationship in the Scandinavian alliance and lead to both more stable and more mutually helpful trade agreements.

Through its membership in international organizations, Denmark wields worldwide influence. The Danish foreign policy of peace and cooperation is transmitted through Denmark's own example—through its financial and technical aid, through its constructive activities, its legislation, and its people.

Many examples of Denmark's humanitarian acts toward other peoples and nations might be cited. Japan has never forgotten the friendship of Denmark during World War II, when the Danes protected those Japanese who escaped from Germany into Denmark and sought refuge until they could get home. Palestinian refugees, since 1948, have received extensive contributions for relief and for education and training programs. Denmark has offered interest-free loans to scores of countries for the purchase of industrial equipment and has furnished aid to destitute Vietnamese. Another worthy Danish project has been the construction of a large demonstration farm in Thailand.

In the field of education, Denmark has opened its doors generously to students from the developing countries, accommodating more than one thousand such students a year. And in order to promote world peace and understanding, the Danes established an international university in north Zealand. This International People's College at Helsingør, founded in 1921, has long been instrumental in promoting international understanding. In an attempt to serve the purpose of developing worldwide peace, it offers students opportunities for developing their personal talents, while at the same time sharing in a fellowship of work and music with students from different nations.

Denmark's many distinctive contributions in the fields of arts, sciences, and literature have been recognized and acclaimed internationally. Hans Christian Andersen's fairy tales have been translated into nearly as many languages as the Bible. Danish silver, porcelain, and furniture are famous in many lands. And what American doesn't appreciate the *aegte* (genuine) Danish cheese, bacon, ham, and even honey!

But while other countries have admired the successful accomplishments of the Danes, so the Danes have shown their admiration of the outstanding achievements of others. The highest Danish order, that of the Order of the Elephant, customarily bestowed on sovereigns and other royal persons, presidents, and distinguished Danes, has been conferred upon four foreign dignitaries: former President Dwight D. Eisenhower and Field Marshall Sir Bernard Montgomery, in 1945, for their distinguished service as leaders in defeating Nazi Germany in World War II and thus liberating Denmark;

Sir Winston Churchill, in 1950; and General Charles de Gaulle, President of France, in 1965.

The Danes have a real and sincere friendship for the United States and for Americans. They feel a kinship with Americans because of the great number of Danes who emigrated to the United States. There are more Danes in the United States than reside now in Denmark. Just the fact that you were born on American soil will open many Danish doors for you.

The close ties between the Danes and Americans are symbolized by the Rebild Fourth of July celebration, which is a remarkable demonstration of international good will. These festivities are held each year in the amphitheater of the Rebild Hills in Jutland in recognition of the significant help provided by the United States in freeing Denmark from the Nazi conquest and providing funds through the Marshall Plan for its postwar recovery. Incidentally, Denmark is one of the few European nations that fully repaid their Marshall Plan loans.

The Danish people are keenly aware of world happenings. Because of its homogeneous population and limited experience with the problems of extremes in size and in social cultures, Denmark as a nation cannot understand, perhaps, the contradictions of larger nations on the political and social scene. But Denmark maintains an attitude of openness and frankness and expresses its opinion through its governmental diplomats, seeking to contribute toward the eventual solution of world problems.

In its unique position as a silent and unbiased referee on the international struggle for world peace, Denmark stretches out a welcoming, open hand to all. Whether the newcomers be refugees or foreign notables, tourists or students, they are treated with respect, friendliness, and helpfulness—gestures that are more influential than money or missions in conveying a country's genuine trust in the implicit goodness of humankind and faith in a happier world society.

The young and the old in Denmark

CHAPTER 6

SOCIAL CONSCIOUSNESS

AS IN MOST COUNTRIES, there is a very close connection in Denmark between economic developments and the introduction of social legislation. Since the 1800s, as industrialization has increased in Denmark, the country has developed many social welfare programs to support the working people.

The earliest of such social laws was enacted through the June Constitution of 1849, which provided public assistance for families in need. The first parliamentary act for workers' protection was passed in 1873, with provisions for restricting the work of children in factories. Later regulations dealt with inspection of hygienic and sanitary conditions, an eight-hour day, and Sunday closings.

Socialized medicine has probably been discussed most often in connection with the "welfare state" of Denmark— criticized, questioned, imitated, and envied. Indeed, the *sygeforsikring* (sickness insurance) has become one of the most comprehensive public health programs in the world. This government-sponsored health insurance covers prenatal care, childbirth, childhood illnesses, adult illness and surgery, hospitalization, dental care, home nursing, convalescence, autopsy, and burial fees. These benefits are paid for by taxes levied on income and collected in the regular income-tax withholding. The employer pays approximately half of the cost and the employee the remainder.

Any resident of Denmark, regardless of occupation or income, enrolls in the *sygeforsikring*. Enrollment is made under one of two categories. Group A includes persons whose incomes are below those of the national average income, about $11,800 for married persons and $8,500 for unmarried. Group B includes those individuals whose income is above this average. Group A members are treated by general practitioners, each member choosing his or her own doctor for a period of one year. Group B members must pay for their own office calls and consultation, but through the local government Group B members are reimbursed for up to 80 percent of the cost of their medical care. However, they may elect to subscribe to private health insurance as well.

Most family physicians in Denmark maintain lists of A and B patients. They generally see the A's in the morning from eight until noon and B's in the afternoon. The morning patients are seen clinic fashion—three to four an hour—while the afternoon patients get, perhaps, an hour of consultation. As a result, some persons prefer to enroll in the B group and pay the extra fee for extra services. But the level of medical skill is high in Denmark, and in all probability the A patient is receiving adequate diagnostic services and treatment in spite of the briefer consultation.

A patient who has a serious illness is sent by the family physician into the hospital for further diagnosis and treatment. While in the hospital, the patient is treated by specialists who practice only in the hospital and are on the hospital staff. The family physician has no privileges in the hospital and loses contact with the hospitalized patient. However, when the patient is discharged, the private doctor receives a complete evaluation, with recommendations for treatment— a service which is of great help in the continuing care of the patient.

Much of the health activity in Denmark is directed toward preventive medicine and the prompt treatment of disabling diseases. For example, early vaccination for common childhood diseases is routine, and free clinics for venereal disease are widely available.

The comprehensive Industrial Insurance Act grants benefits for all job-related injuries and occupational diseases, including treatment and retraining, daily cash benefits, compensation for disability, remuneration to next of kin, and burial costs in case of death.

The Maternity Welfare Act provides for free visits and examinations of expectant mothers by physicians and midwives. Incidentally, the Danish midwife, who plays the same professional role as the physician's assistant in the United States, has been very successful in attending uncomplicated cases of childbirth.

Other legislation goes further in the area of social welfare. The Child and Family Allowance Act gives women medical assistance during pregnancies and free admission to the hospital for delivery, plus an additional maternity leave payment for three months. Maternity welfare centers provide advice on legal, medical, personal, and social matters to both married and unmarried mothers.

Public support for children in the home is given to widows or divorcees for at least six months. The mother receives a tax-free cash allowance for each child under eighteen, though the law demands that the separated parent who does not have the custody of the children contribute a maintenance allowance for the support of his or her children.

Another aspect of the social welfare program is the social pension, which has two principal aims. First, it provides enough money for full support of the individual or couple without additional funds from relatives or other agencies.

And secondly, the agency bears all costs without qualifying conditions. The Pension Law of 1965 states that all Danish citizens who have reached a pensionable age—for men and married women, age sixty-seven, and for single women, age sixty-two—are entitled to the basic retirement pension regardless of other income or capital. This pension is automatically adjusted to the cost of living. In addition, all wage earners receive a supplemental pension after the age of sixty-seven. Disability pensions are also given when the worker's capacity has been reduced by half or more because of physical injuries or mental illness.

Denmark's rising population, with limited land areas in which to contain it, brought about the formation of the Danish Family Planning Association on February 4, 1956. Prior to this, unwanted pregnancies were eliminated by abortion, to the extent that 80 percent of legal abortions were done on married women. Accordingly, the law was further liberalized to provide safe abortions for all women, married and unmarried, and also provided funds to organizations for services in family planning.

Of surprise to the visitor in the public schools are the signs of *tandlaege* (dentist) and *laege* (physician) directing children to their offices and treatment rooms within the school. Preventive dentistry, like preventive medicine, is an important part of the school's health programs. Every school child has a complete dental examination once a year in the school, and appropriate dental treatment is instituted. A school physician also examines each child yearly for physical defects, growth deviation, and disease, and recommends appropriate treatment.

The prisons in Denmark are administered according to the best modern psychological principles. Prisoners are given opportunities for pursuing individual interests, such as painting or woodcarving. Kragskovhede is an example of an open prison, where high walls and ugly enclosures have been abandoned, and probationary leaves and special privileges are accorded to a great degree. Many new rehabilitating treatments are being tried—a far cry from the days when horrendous, life-long torture in the dungeons of a castle was common punishment for the crime, say, of adultery.

When in World War II the German officers saw the new imposing prison structure in the city of Horsens for the first time, they thought it was a castle and immediately commanded occupancy. Disillusioned as to its function, they did not get their wish fulfilled—until the war was over, that is, when many Nazis became permanent "residents" there!

Recognizing the responsibility of the state and community in dealing with children whose parents both work outside the home, Denmark has developed a comprehensive program which is attempting to solve the problem. Administration of child care is performed by regional advisers and local committees responsible to the Directorate of Child and Youth Welfare Services under the Ministry of Family Affairs.

Children between the ages of three and seven are enrolled in *børnehaver* (day nurseries), and children from birth to three years are enrolled in *vuggestuer* (cradle centers).

As in the United States, the number of single mothers in Denmark has been steadily increasing. Taxes are exorbitantly high, especially for the married couple, and housing is more available at less cost for the single person than for the married. These factors have contributed to the problem, creating more single parent families and sending more mothers of young children into the employment field. For this reason, most of the children needing care are those of working mothers, and these families are given preference.

In the *vuggestuer,* each infant is held while being fed,

bathed, and dressed, always by the same person, who acts as a substitute parent. In all-day care, the child is given three meals a day and vitamins. In the infant centers there is one adult for every two babies, while the ratio is one adult to five children in the *børnehaver*. The staff must include teachers who have had three years of practical and theoretical training at a child-care training college. For the preschoolers, lunch usually consists of the appetizing Danish open-faced sandwiches and milk, with snacks of milk or fruit morning and afternoon.

Every day-care center must meet government standards for hygiene, play space, staffing, and program. Hygienic conditions are everywhere in evidence, and such facilities as small toilets, a bathing room, a sick room, a doctor's room, washroom, kitchen, and a playroom for each age group are standard requirements. Infants nap outdoors on covered patios, snuggled warmly in protected cradles, while nursery children sleep on blanketed cots, some of them on doubledeckers. Children are grouped by age, with not more than ten in a group.

And how are these beautiful havens for children supported? The cost is shared by the state, the community, and the parent. The state provides about four-sevenths of the cost; the community and the parent provide the remainder. The total cost amounts to around eighty dollars a month per child, averaging about twenty dollars a month for the parent, based, however, on a sliding scale according to the family income and number of children. Child support from the state pays the parent's share in extremely needy cases.

Many activities and programs are also set up for the school-age child in Denmark. More than two hundred and sixty recreation centers, accommodating sixteen thousand children aged seven to twelve, are open before and after school hours. Hundreds of youth clubs, with a large variety of occupational facilities, and numerous playgrounds and free-time classes are supervised by specially trained recreation directors.

As far as housing is concerned, that problem is of great concern in Denmark as it is elsewhere in the world. But the Danish nation is making an attempt to solve the problem in two ways—by building numerous apartment complexes, and by encouraging the building of small family homes. Everywhere in the outskirts of the larger cities, one sees high-rise structures—many of them built to replace substandard houses for low-income people.

Good housing is also promoted through government grants to architects and home builders and through subsidies to lending institutions, but unfortunately the extremely high taxes and interest rates tend to discourage families from investing in their own separate homes.

Numerous objections are being raised to the towering apartment projects that tend to destroy the *hyggelig* (homey) comfort found in a smaller community. In order to meet the great need for accommodations, the six- to ten-storied apartments have often been built with little heed to garden space and little room for attractive surroundings.

The Dane's love of community fellowship is the chief Danish ingredient for contented living. People are not happy when they are set up in apartments that isolate them and provide no social or recreational facilities. A number of new suburban developments have laid out model centers that do provide such attractions.

Through zoning legislation and regional and local planning committees, the use of land is being restricted to leave room enough for the kind of comfortable living the Danes enjoy. Land planning is based on the prediction that 90 percent of the people will want to live in houses with gardens and that half of this number will have a summer cottage besides. Open spaces, parks, and farmland—and yes, even old villages (under the National Trust)—are being preserved under the plans recommended. Incidentally, the pensioner, the disabled person, and the welfare recipient may also enjoy a week to a month's stay at a garden or beach house. Many small summer cottages, built especially for the needy, are available at low rents.

It was N. F. S. Grundtvig, the famous Danish theologian, who expressed the Danish ideal for social existence—"that few shall have too much and fewer still too little."

It is true that some of the Danes today are not happy in having their needs and comforts automatically provided for. In a letter to the editor of the newspaper *Berlingske Tidende* in March 1974, a reader complained that he would just as soon keep the kroner he earned and pay out of his own pocket the insurance needed for the safety and protection of his family. A polite *"Nej, Tak"* (No, Thanks) headed the article. On the same page was another letter, entitled *"Vaer Stolt af Danmark"* (Be Proud of Denmark). The author of this letter praised the personal concern and care given the old and sick in Denmark compared to that offered in other countries, of which he had visited seventy-five!

By means of its extensive social mindfulness, Denmark has become for some a "security vault" and for others a "blessed state." From birth to death, the Danish citizens are insured for illness, accident, unemployment, pregnancy, old age, poverty, and burial. The law provides it and the state upholds it! The Danish people have been disciplined in the correctness and order of things, and for the most part they enjoy the reasonableness of feeling "safe and sound" as much as they do the "coziness" of their own homes. But the innate initiative and independence of the Danes have in some cases kindled their creative desire to prove themselves capable of serving their own personal needs, spending or saving their own money as they please, for protection or for pleasure, and coming out (as their frugal natures hope) a bit ahead!

Yes, there are those Danes who openly disapprove of the vast sums of money spent on day-care services, rent subsidies, and early pensions given persons on lower income or welfare, and bills are constantly being presented in the *Folketing* for revising health and welfare laws. Some changes will doubtless be forthcoming in the years ahead. A favorite Danish proverb states: *"Pas på ikke at smide barnet ud med badevandet"* (Be careful not to throw the baby out with the bath water). A wise caution, perhaps.

The Grundtvig Church in Copenhagen
Insert: N. F. S. Grundtvig

CHAPTER 7

A CHURCH IN TRANSITION

IN THE NINTH CENTURY A.D., worship of pagan gods was still to be found in the Scandinavian countries—long after Christianity had become widespread in most of the rest of Europe. South of Denmark lay the large Christian kingdom of France, where the mighty emperor Louis I reigned. He had forced the Saxons to accept Christianity and looked for ways of doing the same to the Danes, who resisted conversion.

When King Harald Bluetooth of Jutland asked for help in becoming reinstated in his kingdom, the emperor agreed to help him if he in turn would be baptized. Agreeing to these terms, the king accepted Christianity, and when he returned to his homeland, a Benedictine monk by the name of Ansgar accompanied him. Arriving in South Jutland in 827 as the "Apostle of the North," Ansgar was the first person to bring Christianity to the shores of Denmark.

Under the protection of King Harald, Ansgar began his task of converting the antagonistic Danes. He established a church at Hedeby, now in Schleswig, and later started the first church in Denmark, in the town of Ribe on the western coast of Jutland. To this day, many mission hotels in Denmark bear Ansgar's name, as do many in Sweden and Norway, where Ansgar also preached.

Bishops sent back to Denmark by King Canute during his

reign over England and Scandinavia helped to spread the Christian religion. But the church was to become a more effective influence under Canute the Saint (1080-1086) and Erik the Kindhearted (1095-1103).

Canute the Saint worked diligently to strengthen the church, but he made the grave error of attempting another Viking expedition to reconquer England. His subjects rebelled and finally assassinated him as he knelt in prayer at the church in Odense. He was later canonized through the persistent efforts and pleas of his brother, Erik the Kindhearted. The Church of Saint Canute in Odense, where he lies buried, was named in his honor.

Under Erik the Kindhearted's reign, the church became financially independent. The king established the system of tithing, which considerably increased the wealth of the church and led to the building of more costly church edifices, of stone instead of wood. Some of the great Danish cathedrals date from this time.

The Reformation penetrated the Scandinavian countries in the early 1500s. The introduction of Protestantism was supported by burghers and peasants and by devout priests who had become followers of Martin Luther. King Frederik I (1523-1533), who became quite religious in his later years, strongly promoted the establishment of the Lutheran Church. He allowed the leading Danish religious reformer, Hans Tavsen, to preach in the church at Viborg and ordered many Catholic churches in the region destroyed, despite violent protests.

It was King Christian III (1534-1559), son of Frederik I, who established the state Lutheran Church in Denmark. With the support of the *Rigsraad*—his advising council of lay members—the king ordered all Catholic property turned over to the crown and declared the Lutheran Church the national church of Denmark with the king as its head. Under one of the king's advisers, Johan Bugenhagen, a new church constitution was worked out, and the hierarchy so long present in the early church was eliminated.

From 1660 to 1849, a period of absolute monarchy in Denmark, all citizens were compelled to profess the Lutheran faith. The King's Law of 1665 declared that the king himself must adhere to the Confession of Augsburg and "maintain the citizens of the country in the same pure and uncorrupted faith." Declaring the king to be "the supreme and highest head" in the realm of religion, Christian V's Danish Law of 1683 stated that "the evangelical Lutheran faith should, within the king's realms and possessions, alone be permitted."

Compulsory religious affiliation continued, generally, until 1849, when *Grundloven* granted complete religious freedom to every citizen of Denmark. The law stipulated that all persons could enjoy civil and political rights regardless of their religious beliefs, and it gave permission for people to form separate religious groups and assemble to worship according to individual religious convictions.

The Lutheran Church had been greatly influenced during the early nineteenth century by theologian N.F.S. Grundtvig. He believed that Christian belief should be based on the Apostles' Creed, the sacraments of baptism and Holy Communion, and on the Lord's Prayer, rather than on the Scriptures. He emphasized the simple life of joy and song as expressed through the many beautiful hymns he wrote. Grundtvig influenced both the religious and cultural life of his day. The church service became less orthodox and more sacramental in nature, and it was chiefly due to Grundtvigian impact that religious freedom was eventually introduced in 1849.

Søren Kierkegaard was another prominent figure of the

nineteenth century. A philosopher and theologian, he has often been called "the father of existentialism." His chief concern was for the individual's existence, which, he believed, was a subjective one—an existence for which each person must assume full responsibility and hence feel guilt. Kierkegaard became violently opposed to the official Christendom of his day, and his views, though understood by only a few, have had a profound effect on the scholars and theologians all over the world.

During the later half of the nineteenth century, the Lutheran Church became more pietistic in nature—ecclesiastical and sacramental—adopting a form that it has since then generally maintained.

Freedom of worship also brought in other denominations and freer thought and expression. There is even now a tugging at the ties that bind religion to the state. One wonders how long it will be before those ties will be broken, although, as one theologian wrote recently, that severance may be the death of the church. To break away from the support of the state too quickly may leave the church severely deprived and floundering, without a penny or a promise.

Today there is complete religious freedom in Denmark, and all people may decide for themselves whether or not to belong to the Lutheran Church. Whereas formerly the church was designated as the "state" church, it is now called *Folkekirken,* or the people's church, still sometimes referred to as the National Church. The distinction is made in order to emphasize the freedom of the people in their choice of belief, yet to denote that the majority of the citizens have elected the Lutheran faith and church in preference to others.

Although the Constitution of 1849 states that "a constitution for the National Church of Denmark shall be prescribed by law," the Danish church does not yet have a constitution of its own. It has no head bishop or moderator who represents the church at international church councils, and no synodical organization. The Minister for Ecclesiastical Affairs in the *Folketing* administers politically the affairs of the church. Under this ministry, there are ten bishops assigned to ten dioceses and ninety-eight deaneries supervising about twenty-three hundred churches and eighteen hundred active clergy. The clergy and the parish councils, elected by congregation members, are responsible for their individual parishes.

The state does contribute substantially to the support of the church through yearly grants, and it levels a membership tax which is included in the annual income tax of every Danish citizen. Without much trouble, non-members of the Lutheran church may be exempted from paying church tax. The state pays the pastor's salary, but the local church is responsible to some extent for maintenance and building projects. Each parish church may select its own pastor and plan its individual form of service and program.

Most of the theologians receive their training at the universities in Århus and Copenhagen, even though the church now ordains non-theologians because of the shortage of pastors. In 1947, the *Folketing* passed a law permitting women to be ordained and, since that time, women have entered the ministerial field.

Heretofore, the teaching of religion in the public schools has been compulsory and according to Lutheran doctrine. Because of much controversy, the courses now consist of the history of the church and a study of all religions, in order to avoid indoctrination. This change is leading to renewed interest in providing religious instruction in the Sunday School, which had been almost extinct in most churches.

School and national holidays in Denmark still include those in the church calendar. In other words, "holy days" are holidays.

Of the entire population of Denmark, about 92 percent belong to the *Folkekirken*. Of the other eight nationally accepted denominations in the country, the Roman Catholics claim the largest number, about twenty-two thousand members, the Baptists about ten thousand, and the Methodists five thousand.

Church attendance in Denmark has been noticeably poor in recent years, diminishing gradually since World War II. (During the worrisome war years the people sought spiritual support, and churches were packed.) Today attendance varies from .5 percent of the membership in metropolitan churches to 15 percent of the membership in rural churches. Of course, considering the fact that nearly the entire population of Denmark is included in the membership, that count is not as shocking as it at first may seem. The wide variation in attendance according to area and location of the churches also must be considered.

In the great cathedrals of Copenhagen and Århus, for example, the meager attendance at church services is quite noticeable. The central urban population, as in many American cities, is moving out into suburbs and rural areas, where new housing developments and huge apartment complexes are available. A number of architecturally unique churches have been built in many of these sections, and young enthusiastic pastors claim to have active and interested congregations.

By contrast, the small white-washed village churches with their stepped roofs—so prevalent on the Danish landscape—may or may not attract a Sunday audience. At the largest village church in Denmark, Vestervig Church—on the far western coast of Jutland—about two hundred persons can be counted in attendance on a Sunday morning. Well-attended also is the village church at Udby, birthplace of Grundtvig. Here the church bell rings out as it has for more than a hundred years, calling the faithful parishioners to services. This was the setting that inspired Grundtvig to write the famous poem set to music, *"Kirkeklokker, ej til Hovedsteder"* (Church Bells, Not of the City).

Currently, it is true, many young people, as well as their parents, are saying casually that they do not need the church. Yet those same persons will add, "Baptism, confirmation, and weddings are fun occasions. So is Christmas. We like the singing, the presents, and celebration." The Danes you meet may tell you bluntly, "We don't go to church." Most of them will probably not know the significance of the religious holidays, and *"Skål"* has taken the place of saying grace at mealtime.

Many Danes feel that the church, as it is today, serves no purpose. A majority are still baptized, confirmed, and married in the church, although fewer than formerly. Only about 77 percent of the babies are being baptized. Yet one may be quite impressed with the throngs of persons attending an Easter concert or cantata in Vor Frue Kirke in Copenhagen or a midsummer concert of sacred music given by organ, orchestra, and the 150-voice Jutland choir in the Thisted Church in Jutland.

As more than four hundred thousand people do gather for worship each Sunday in the churches in Denmark, they do so in widely different types of structures—the village church, the cathedral, and the modern church, each attractive and unique. Some have organs dating from the sixteenth and seventeenth centuries—and the eighteen hundred churches built originally between A.D. 1100 and 1250 have been re-

stored and are kept in excellent repair. Neighboring ceme-
teries, like colorful flower gardens, are reverently tended.
Anyone who travels in Denmark should definitely visit a
number of Danish churches, since they serve not only as
places of worship but often as unique museums of art.

New kinds of services are being tried in various church
congregations. These innovative services have proved to be
quite successful and are especially well accepted by the young
people. The new Ecumenical Center at Århus University is
probably the most experimental and different. Non-denomi-
national and international in character, this Christian center
organizes and promotes group conferences, camps, and workshops not only in Denmark but also, in cooperation with
ecumenical groups in other countries—Switzerland, Itaiy,
Austria, France, Finland, and Sweden.

Activities within the church are limited. Only a few have
women's associations or social groups. Boy Scouts, Girl
Scouts, YMCA, YWCA, and similar organizations may be
sponsored by the church but do not come under its auspices.
However, the church strongly supports local and foreign
missions plus similar charitable endeavors. In 1974 more
than half a million dollars was donated to the church's
"Bread for the World" project.

In St. Olai's Church in Helsingør, above the entrance to
the altar, is seen a most unusual picture, dating from the
seventeenth century. Observed from one side, it shows
Jesus Christ on the cross; yet, surprisingly, when seen from
the other side, it is a picture of the Ascension. When viewed
from the center, in the transition, the portrayal seems slightly
blurred. Perhaps the church in Denmark is at the present
time in the transitional stage. Within the Danish church
today, there is apparently a real need for religious expression
and inspiration, though the spirit for active participation

seems to lie dormant, waiting for a leadership and a purpose to guide it out of a slumbering static state and provide a creatively motivated direction. Since Denmark has always been keenly aware of its weaknesses as well as its strengths, it is fairly certain that it will always appreciate that rich and sustaining religious heritage so faithfully preserved and restored through its many churches, and that it will imperceptibly change and move, as in the picture, toward the vision of a new and more promising day in its religious life.

The old ways: a town drummer
The new ways: newspapers and magazines for every taste

CHAPTER 8

A COMMUNICATIVE SOCIETY

A LOOK AT THE communications media of the Danish press, Radio Denmark, and the Danish film industry gives a person real insight into Danish ways.

Few nations of the Western world can boast as many newspaper readers (or, for that matter, television viewers) per capita as Denmark. All Danes can read, and nearly every adult regularly reads a newspaper.

The press to the Danes means the daily newspapers—a general forum of public information and debate. There are sixty-two dailies, with total circulation of about 1,750,000 —the largest dailies being *Aktuelt, Berlingske Tidende,* and *Politiken* in Copenhagen and *Jyllands-Posten* in Århus.

The content of the newspapers is moderately lively but by no means lurid. The tabloids, of course, use an easy-to-read format and are profusely illustrated. Note, for example, the extremely popular midday tabloids, *B.T.* (circulation 217,000) and *Extrabladet* (222,000)—and now the new form of the Sunday tabloid, *Aktuelt,* put out by the Social Democrat Party press.

While there are no markedly "quality" newspapers, most of the publications tend toward presenting a good balance of hard news, background information, and commentary— concentrating on a range of interests. They shun both sensationalism and showy erudition. You'll find no banner headlines in Denmark proclaiming events of crime and violence.

Politically, most Danish newspapers have clearly defined political views, even though they try to give space to a wide range of information and a variety of opinion. Nine of them are conservative and traditional, but seven of them are radical and do not hesitate to express ideas that oppose those of political incumbents. Another seven are Social Democrat papers, owned by the trade unions and, of course, linked to the Social Democrat Party. *Land og Folk* belongs to the Communist Party. There are seven newspapers that are definitely nonpartisan. Notable among these are *Børsen* (Stock Exchange), a paper for people in industry and commerce, and *Kristelig Dagblad,* which presents both domestic and foreign news, strives for a Christian interpretation, and pleads the cause of cooperation.

Another nonpartisan but politically inspired newssheet is Copenhagen's *Information,* dedicated to the objective of defining issues and attitudes. It began as a hunted underground publication during the German occupation and emerged as an independent, daily newspaper on the day of liberation in May 1945. Its unique feature today is that it is owned entirely by its staff, from editor-in-chief to janitorial workers—a supreme example of industrial democracy.

In spite of the wide coverage of international news in Danish papers, you will notice that domestic news predominates; in fact, news about Danes themselves, particularly in the provinces, occupies a considerable amount of space. There is much friendly material of family interest, a generous sprinkling of funny cartoons, and smiling commentary. There are columns playing up items of historical interest (events that occurred fifty, one hundred, or two hundred years ago on the same date); special space for honored citizens who are celebrating their fiftieth, sixtieth, seventieth, eightieth, ninetieth, or one hundredth birthdays; and children's pages with stories, puzzles, jokes, and announcements of youngsters' contests and other activities. Frank commentaries, extensive previews, and illustrated, often severe, program critiques of television, radio, and stage shows occupy good-sized sections of most general newspapers. The opinions of columnists are apparently highly regarded.

The advertising section, as in most countries, makes fascinating and informative reading. You may be surprised to see display ads—rather than classifieds—used for "Help Wanted" advertisements. Among the long, long list of classified ads you will find the common request, "Male (or female) companion needed. Object matrimony."

For foreign news, the Danish papers are chiefly dependent on the various news agencies, while the foreign press is generally served by the Foreign Ministry Press and Information Department.

Historically, the Danes are accustomed to reading their news. Danish newssheets go back as far as 1666, and four of the existing newspapers were founded in the eighteenth century—Copenhagen's *Berlingske Tidende* and the three *Stiftstidende* of Ålborg, Århus, and Odense.

Because of the marked trend toward local monopolies and fewer but larger newspapers, there is also pronounced inclination toward concentration of ownership. For example, one family business publishes *Berlingske Tidende* (a morning paper), the *Berlingske Aftenavis* (an afternoon), the tabloid *B.T.* and *Jydske Tidende* (a Jutland paper)—all of which gives the company control of 23.5 percent of the combined daily circulation in Denmark. In addition, the family receives the proceeds from a large printing works, two weeklies, and other enterprises. Another family owns a chain of six medium-sized liberal papers. In fact, 56 percent of total newspaper circulation is concentrated in four companies.

However, economically and financially, the picture for the Danish press has not been too favorable during the past few decades. Most small newspapers have faced serious dilemmas, and some publications are heavily subsidized.

Two things you will immediately notice about Denmark's radio and television programs. One is the absence of commercials. The other is their great popularity. Even when guests are present, the family sets are likely to be turned on and the programs enjoyed whenever they are available. While Danish radio appears to be in its golden age of achievement, Danish television is merely in its adolescence. There is only one channel, which has limited program time. Perhaps those facts in themselves account for television's great popularity.

All radio and television broadcasting is handled by Radio Denmark—an independent, public organization established in 1925 and now vested with sole rights under the Broadcasting Act of 1959. It is directly responsible to the Danish Ministry of Cultural Affairs. The eighteen-member Radio Council is the unit that lays down the policies and principles of the airwaves and oversees program content. Two of the council members are appointed by the Minister of Cultural Affairs; one person is a radio engineer appointed by the Minister of Public Works; ten people represent the viewing and listening public and are appointed by the parliament; and five represent the political parties that are represented on the Parliamentary Finance Committee.

The standards for quality programs are generally high in Denmark—notably, perhaps, in the areas of drama, ballet, and music. Handled by its own expert staff of writers, editors, camera operators, actors, directors, and special effects crew, the television theater now provides in Denmark—as in the United States—real competition for the legitimate playhouses. The members of the Danish public by this time expect to see, in the comfort of their own homes, such masterpieces as the classic Strindberg play *The Father* or Ibsen's *A Doll's House*.

However, the television programs in Denmark (including news) are not limited to Danish productions. A great many popular shows from other countries are run—chiefly selections from England and the United States—using Danish subtitles.

The Voice of Denmark (short-wave service) is handled by a separate department. For forty-five minutes each day a program in Danish—as well as a thirty-minute program in English and Spanish—is beamed to North America, the Far East, southern Asia, Africa, South America, and Greenland. The Danish program emphasizes news, commentaries, and talk shows—mostly about developments in Denmark. The foreign language programs try to present an unbiased, overall picture of Danish life and culture.

It is good to know that in spite of the limitations of the electronics industry, the Danes do not feel cheated in their radio-television programs. In addition to their own shows and re-broadcasts, people in two-thirds of the country may watch and listen to Swedish or German programs, depending on their proximity to Sweden or Germany.

Bear in mind that no commercial advertising is allowed on Denmark's airwaves. If there are no sponsors, who provides the support for the programs? The public does, of course. Each person or family owning a radio or television set must pay an annual license fee, about fifty dollars—more for color television. But certainly no complaints are heard on this score from the Danes.

It might be said that the idea for the Danish film industry began with a funeral—a royal funeral—in the year 1906. At the beginning of that year, Ole Olsen (1863-1943) filmed the funeral of King Christian IX. His work was received so well that Olsen, that very year, founded an industry destined to become one of the most successful businesses in Denmark. Olsen's firm was the famous *Nordisk Films Kompagni,* of which he later would be the managing editor. By the end of 1906, his company had released thirty-two Danish films.

In all fairness, it should be mentioned that the very first Danish film was made in 1898 by court photographer Peter Elfelt—a documentary of the royal family. Perhaps it is significant that these two early attempts were documentaries —an area that has brought considerable acclaim to Danish films. But more of that later.

For so small a country, Denmark made an astounding number of silent films in the twenty-five years between 1906 and 1931—1,627 of them! By far the most of them (1,105) were made between 1911 and 1921. After that, the demand began to taper off until the arrival of "sound" at the end of the next decade.

The first sound film in Denmark was made in 1931. It was based on the famous story *Praesten i Vejby,* by Steen Steensen Blicher, telling of the miscarriage of justice in a small Danish village.

Denmark has distinguished itself in melodramatic films, and it has also attracted favorable attention in its filming of the literary story, especially the kind calling for crowds and mass effects like Gerhart Hauptmann plays.

However, it is chiefly the consolidated documentary industry that has been the attention-getter in Danish film production. This has been true even though the language barrier has been a definite problem. Theodor Christensen is considered one of the best documentarists or producers of social films. Although two of his creations might be considered controversial—*Tre År Efter* (Three Years After), concerning the German occupation, and *Café Paradis,* an exposé of alcoholism—they are generally pronounced excellent.

One of the documentaries received with the most enthusiasm was *En Ny Virkelighed* (A New Reality). This 1963 film, produced for Dansk Kulturfilm and International Council for Education Films, explained Niels Bohr's theory of nuclear physics.

Numerous famous Danish personages from the film industry might be named, but only a few standouts can be mentioned here. One of the most famous directors was Carl Th. Dreyer (1889-1968). He is famous for such productions as *Ordet, Gertrud, Jeanne d'Arc,* and *Vredens Dag* (Day of Wrath).

One outstanding couple, Astrid and Bjarne Henning-Jensen, worked together as directors in many films. But Astrid's own production entitled *Paw,* about a young black boy and a poacher, became a two-time prize-winner internationally. It is interesting to note that since 1940 Denmark has had six other successful women directors in addition to Astrid Henning-Jensen.

During the 1960s director Henning Carlsen (born in 1927) came into prominence. His first artistic success, produced in 1966, was undoubtedly *Sult* (Hunger), a film based on the Norwegian novel by Knut Hamsun. The fact that Carlsen integrated three languages, with apparently no difficulty in communication, added new directions in Scandinavian cooperation as well as in artistic possibilities.

The old farmstead
Insert: Today's specially bred Danish bacon pig

CHAPTER 9

AN INDUSTRIOUS PEOPLE

THERE ARE TWO general factors that influence the kind and amount of goods produced in Denmark. The first is the country's natural asset of plenty of agricultural land, which automatically gives Denmark its reputation of being a land of farms. The second factor, Denmark's lack of natural resources, such as minerals and oil, has forced the country to import raw materials and increase manufacturing enterprises in order to meet the demand of a more industrialized society.

For many generations, the fertile parts of Zealand, Funen, and Jutland had been exploited to the full, and as early as the nineteenth century it was apparent that additional agricultural land was sorely needed. The heath lands of Jutland, which had been ruined agriculturally in the Middle Ages by the field-burning method of farming, were the only lands available. Denmark owes a great debt of gratitude to Enrico Dalgas, a second-generation Swiss immigrant, who formed the Heath Society in 1886 to reclaim large areas of western and northern Jutland by deep plowing, liming, and reforestation with windbreaks, thereby converting the wild moorland of Jutland to fertile dairy farms.

Almost 75 percent of the land area of Denmark is now devoted to agriculture. It is divided into approximately one hundred and forty thousand farms, more of which are privately owned than in any other European country. However, the number of smaller farms has been decreasing, and the size of the average farm has increased from twenty-five acres to forty-seven acres. In addition, many more farms than formerly are larger than one hundred acres in size.

The Danes have excelled in farm production for many reasons, including the founding of cooperatives and the development of product specialization.

It is not surprising that Denmark should be the country that established the first cooperative dairy. The Danes have a social nature, they care about one another, and they are enterprising. These are the characteristics that led them out of an economic dilemma in the late 1800s into a program of self-sustaining, productive management. With the drop in grain prices on the international market at that time and the plummeting of farmers' profits, it was obvious that some other means of livelihood must be found. Small dairy farmers could not compete with the large commercial dairies, and they sorely needed more cattle and equipment.

An innovative young man by the name of Stilling Andersen, who had attended agricultural school at Ladelund, was eager to try a radical organizational experiment in his home town. He suggested that all the farmers send the milk from their herds to a central creamery for processing into butter and that an assembly be formed among the farmers, giving each person one vote and the right to be heard. A contract of joint ownership was drawn up and a loan made to enable the group to buy the necessary equipment. And on June 10, 1882, in Hjedding, Jutland, the first cooperative dairy was in operation. If you wish, you may visit the creamery, which is now on display in the outdoor Hjerl Heath Museum. Its original machinery is still in good working order.

The cooperative movement spread quickly throughout

Denmark, and by 1888 there were about three hundred and fifty cooperative dairies in existence. By 1890, there were seven hundred, and today 95 percent of the more than two hundred thousand Danish dairies are members of a cooperative dairy.

In 1887, a few years after Andersen's initial step, a cooperative bacon association was founded by Lars Peter Bojsen, a schoolteacher and farmer who lived near Horsens. As cooperatives flourished, both bacon and butter improved markedly in quality, winning prizes as well as higher prices for their excellence. By 1900, these products made up Denmark's principal export commodities.

Next, egg production became a rapidly growing, cooperative industry. Danish eggs are graded and marketed cooperatively through the Egg Export Association and its nearly eight hundred branches. Every egg is tested for quality and stamped with the individual producer's identification and the date, so that the bad ones can be traced back to the farm from which they came. If there is anything rotten in Denmark, it won't be the eggs!

Actually, the original cooperatives in Denmark were the credit organizations, formed in rural communities in the middle of the nineteenth century to allow farmers to find low-interest money for buying cattle, machinery, and land. The first retail cooperative was organized by Dean Hans Christian Sonne in the small town of Thisted in northern Jutland in 1851. From this simple beginning, a network of more than two thousand retail cooperative societies has sprung up.

The most fundamental principle of the cooperative movement was that of "self-government by its members." From this basic concept has come the practice of economic democracy, avoiding social and political distinctions among the

members. A second principle in the cooperative movement
is the open intake of new members as opposed to a "closed"
cooperation or shop. Anyone who is qualified may join. A
third basic principle is an economic one—the profits are
distributed to the members of the cooperative according to
their individual production, rather than equally.

There are at least six hundred major kinds of cooperative
societies in Denmark, with branches numbering in the thousands for each one. In addition to the dairy cooperatives and
others just mentioned, there are those that raise and export
seed and potatoes and those that market garden and horti-
cultural products. The Danish fisheries have formed cooperatives for marketing their famous herring, halibut, and cod-
fish. There are cooperative banks, insurance companies, and
sanitarium associations, cooperative colleges, bakeries, and
fuel and housing associations, and scores of others—all of
which provide commodities or services to their members.

The spirit of the modern farmer was exemplified by people
like Bent Christensen, who helped develop product specialization—the second important factor influencing the
success of Danish agriculture. When Christensen came home
to Vangstrup, Sjaelland, in 1957, after finishing his agricultural training, he had decided that things could not go on
in the old-fashioned way. Specialization in farm products
was the only solution to the small farmer's problems. By
consolidating several farms and making table chickens and
ducks his specialty items, Christensen was able to streamline
the rearing and feeding operations, decrease the number of
workers to one-half, and triple the efficiency of each worker.

Between 1958 and 1967, the number of persons engaged
in agriculture in Denmark dropped nearly 50 percent, while
the industrial labor force rose 20 percent. Income from agricultural products rose only 2 percent; income from industry

went up 79 percent. Yet the amount of agricultural production as a whole in Denmark could still meet the food requirements of some 15 million people and allow two-thirds of the farm products to be exported to other countries.

Of all the major industries in Denmark, the iron and steel industry ranks first, accounting for about a third of the total industrial output and employing about a third of the labor force. Danish iron and steel companies produce machines, instruments, electronic equipment, mechanical parts, and diesel engines.

Shipbuilding is a long-established Danish craft, and Denmark has the reputation of being one of the world's leading shipbuilders. Experts from Viking times, the Danes build more and more ships in new shapes and all sizes, from small plastic dinghies to tankers weighing more than a quarter of a million tons. They build ferries with a capacity of a thousand people and four hundred cars and turn out well-designed marine engines and equipment. In fact, Danish shipbuilders have supplied 30 percent of all heavily powered motor ships now sailing.

Another large industry, which now accounts for 17 percent of the labor force, is food processing. This includes beet mills; canneries for meat, fruit, vegetables, milk, and fish; breweries for beer; and liquor and akvavit distilleries. A surprise to many people is the number of sugar refineries located in southern Denmark, mostly on the islands of Lolland and Langeland.

Not so surprising is the fact that the making of beer is truly a Danish art. The Carlsberg Breweries not only provide a refreshing and popular beverage, but also contribute with every glass of beer to the artistic culture and to the advancement of science in Denmark. The original brewery owner, J. C. Jacobsen, set up a trust fund through the

Carlsberg Foundation, whose funds are used to subsidize art museums, purchase paintings and sculpture, and provide grants to scientists and institutions for scientific research. Denmark is the only country in the world in which the price of a glass of beer helps to support art and science.

The fishing industry will always be a stable one, as long as the Danish seas and waters are not polluted by atomic waste or other substances. Denmark has about twelve thousand fishermen, who are catching fish both for home use and export purposes. Fish are exported from Denmark as fresh, canned, frozen, or smoked products.

Other large Danish industries include the manufacturing of paper, textiles, furniture, cement, clothing, and pharmaceutical products.

The world's largest supply of insulin comes from Denmark. With this significant contribution and other firsts in related fields, it's no wonder that Denmark's chemical, plastics, and pharmaceutical industry is gaining international prominence! The Novo Insulin factory (handsomely designed by architect Arne Jacobsen) is located just north of Copenhagen.

Danfoss, begun by engineer Mads Clausen in a small wooden building on his farm on the island of Als, is today a world-renowned organization and one of Denmark's largest industrial plants. This huge corporation manufactures automatic valves, controls, hydraulic components, and compressors for heaters, refrigerating units, motors, and machines. An international corporation, it maintains subsidiaries in six countries, branches in fourteen countries, and trade relations with one hundred countries.

The total manufacturing production in Denmark amounts to approximately 10 billion dollars annually. In all, there are nearly seven thousand manufacturing enterprises in Denmark, employing some four hundred thousand workers at established places of at least six employees (distinguishing industry from handicraft shops, where fewer are employed). About 75 percent employ fewer than five hundred workers, and the majority of these employ around one hundred.

The Danes like to develop things that are new and unusual, and their industrial enterprises reflect this spirit. Unique bus-stop shelters, shaped like half an igloo, are seen today all over Denmark. They were designed by Poul Cadovius of the CADAMUS firm that also constructs some of the large and handsome *idraetshaller* (sports halls) so prevalent throughout the country.

Love of the innovative has further resulted in the CADA-MUS firm's securing a world patent for a device that looks like a child's jack but that ties metal piping into attractive, geometrical, domed figures of all sizes, to be used in the construction of factories, gymnasiums, swimming halls, and innumerable smaller objects. It is called "Abstracta."

The biggest single new industrial enterprise, one that is sure to affect Denmark's economy, is the acquisition of oil from the North Sea. The Danish Underground Consortium, after ten years of offshore exploration, has succeeded in bringing oil from the Dan oil field, 125 miles west of Esbjerg. Hopes are for oil production of five hundred thousand tons a year—only 3 percent of Denmark's consumption. But since the quality of oil is excellent, the price for the oil from the Danish sector may bring as much as 350 million dollars.

Other upcoming projects that should influence Denmark's industrial economy are the proposed construction of a bridge between Zealand and Funen, to be completed in 1982 at a cost of about 500 million dollars and plans for a new airport at Saltholm, scheduled for completion in 1985 at more than 600 million dollars. Concurrently, a tunnel between Helsingør and Helsingborg, and a tunnel and bridge from Copenhagen to Malmø, Sweden, are also expected to be in the making, the cost to be shared with Sweden.

Contrary to the beliefs of most Americans, Denmark does not have a socialist economy. That is, private ownership, development, and control of industry are present throughout Denmark. It is true that the state runs the postal telegraph, cable radio, television, and mass transit services, and that the telephone company is owned and managed by the state and cities jointly. But business and manufacturing enterprises are all privately owned, just as in the United States.

Through many years, Denmark has proven to the world that it can produce almost anything, possibly because it has been endowed with one valuable natural resource—the Danes themselves! The only obstacle they fear is that their earnest endeavors will be for nought. As Piet Hein says:

THE STATE

Nature, our father and mother,
gave us all we have got.
The state, our elder brother,
swipes the lot.

Traditionally, the Danes have high standards of quality and workmanship. They train their workers well in preservice apprenticeship and on-the-job reschooling—whether in farming, crafts, science, or manufacturing. Add their inventive ideas in design, their vigorous spirit of competition, and their pride in a finished product, and you will recognize them as a progressive and industrious people in an advancing industrialized nation.

Newly-graduated students celebrating
with traditional dance in Copenhagen

CHAPTER 10

EDUCATION FOR ALL

A LITTLE WOMAN eighty-six years old is enrolled in a two-weeks' course at the Pensionists High School in Jutland. This school, the first of its kind in Denmark, opened its doors in 1971 and immediately filled its enrollment to capacity for a series of short courses. Fru Karen Hardis, the oldest student, is enthusiastic about returning to school. Proud of her eight children, twenty grandchildren, and twenty great-grandchildren, she has much in common with four other great-grandmothers and ten additional spirited members of the class, whose ages range from sixty to eighty-six.

Lifelong opportunities for learning are open to every person in literate, enlightened Denmark. All citizens may avail themselves of training or education suited to their individual needs and abilities. Young children can be enrolled in infant classes from the time they are born, and great-grandparents may attend evening classes with teenagers or sign up for courses designed for senior citizens.

While centers for children below the age of six are administered by the social welfare division of the government, most schools are under the auspices of the Ministry of Education. All public schools, from kindergarten through college, are supported in full by the state and are therefore free to all students. The private schools may receive up to 80 percent of their operating expenses from the government, while many adult education programs and specialized schools are maintained by local communities or industries.

The prevailing atmosphere of Danish schools is one of happiness. For example, "Shall we sing for you?" is a question you very likely would hear if you were to visit a typical primary class in Denmark today. The spontaneity and friendliness of the children, reflected in this question, may be the key to the educational philosophy and purpose of all schools in Denmark.

The Danes seem to apply to education the *livslyst* (joy of living) that characterizes the prime objective of their existence. The aim of education in Denmark is to provide the best development of the personality and potential of every student in a pleasant environment. In the words of one teacher, "Our aim is to make every child *happy* to go to school." Evidence of this goal is seen in all aspects of education—in the school buildings themselves, in the curriculum, and in the teachers.

In the overall educational picture, the elementary school —now kindergarten through grade ten—stands out as the area undergoing the most radical transformation. The buildings themselves have a new look. In the designs of the modern schools, Danish architecture has produced structures that are both functional and attractive. At the Vangebo School at Solrød, for instance, you will see a separate building—or school home—for each class. And in a Copenhagen suburb, at the beautiful, rambling Tinbjergskole, you'll observe a huge, domed athletic building that resembles a college coliseum.

Typically, the wide, picture-windowed corridors face pleasant open courtyards planted with flowers and shrubs—a perfect setting for one or two pieces of artistic sculpture. Paved playgrounds, separate gymnasiums, swimming pools, multipurpose rooms, audiovisual auditoriums, inviting libraries, hobby rooms, and teachers' lounges are some of the enhancing features of these modern elementary schools. Visitors also notice immediately the signs in each building directing children to the offices of dentist and physician.

Decorative works from famous artists—murals, paintings, tapestries, sculpture—adorn the Danish schools. The state art fund endorses and supports these adornments as part of the enrichment program considered an essential component of educational experience.

The curriculum of these schools is also becoming more child-oriented, shifting from the traditional, formal instruction to a program of related activities and practical learning. This modification may perhaps coincide with the introduction of more kindergartens into the public schools. Observing that learning can be fun and that children learn best through active group participation, school administrators are favoring a more informal approach in a relaxed environment.

An elementary school teacher in Denmark follows his or her class, teaching the basic subjects, from the first through the seventh grade. Then the teacher starts with a new class in grade one. When told that in the United States a child usually has a different teacher every year, a first-grade teacher in one Copenhagen school looked amazed. "What a shame! Why, who gets to know the child?" The Danish teacher aims to discover not only a child's successes and failures but also the reasons behind them. "The child must have one person to whom he or she can turn," explained the teacher.

A favorite subject in the elementary school is *håndværk* (handcraft). Each child masters some skill in sewing, knitting, or embroidery—subjects taught in every class from the second grade on. And children sing the simple folk songs and hymns of their land and church in their daily music class. In grades four, five, and six, they begin their study of English and German, learning to converse rather fluently in these foreign languages.

The sequential system beyond grade seven has always been a complex one in Denmark. Before 1969, students were placed, selectively, into one of two narrow tracts—either the three-year *real klasser,* leading to university preparatory work, or the continuing grades of eight, nine, and ten, providing vocationally slanted courses. Another option for students was to drop out of school after the seventh grade, and many youngsters did just that—especially those who felt stigmatized as academic failures because they were compelled to take the trade courses.

However, the education law of 1969 effected several changes. School attendance had been compulsory in Denmark since 1814, when elementary schools were established throughout the country, and children between the ages of seven and fourteen were required to attend the primary school. The 1969 law made the ninth grade mandatory and school attendance compulsory to age sixteen.

In order to provide a greater choice of subjects and more opportunity for individual pursuits, the curriculum for the upper grades has been revised. In the fall of 1971, an education commission presented a plan for an integrated program for grades one through seven and a graduated, two-level program of instruction for grades eight, nine, and ten. During these three years, subjects are now presented on two levels of difficulty. Students select for themselves the courses they feel are appropriate to their abilities and interests, taking mostly required courses but also a number of electives. An optional final exam is given at the end of the ninth or tenth year, based on subjects the student chooses to be tested on.

Using the results of these exams as guides, students now choose either to attend the academic-oriented *gymnasium* (grades eleven, twelve, and thirteen) by passing the required *realeksamen* or to continue their education in one of the youth schools, technical or training schools, business-secretarial schools, or one of the many trade-apprenticeship schools. If prepared, a student may take the *realeksamen* as early as the end of the ninth year.

Thus the Danish elementary school is now providing more program flexibility for all students and more options to choose from.

The school day is a short one. For children through grade three, dismissal is at noon or at one. For the remainder, dismissal time is two in the afternoon, and students attend classes in their special interests after school. The subjects in the *fritidsklasser* (free-time classes)—such as drama, chess, art, Spanish, photography, handball, orchestra, tennis—are explored individually or in groups, and they are sometimes designed to prepare young people for competitive meets. In 1971 there were more than fifty such groups in Århus alone, staffed by volunteer teachers or persons hired by educational or private organizations.

There are thirty teacher-training colleges, *seminarier*, for educating teachers of the primary schools. Admission is by written and oral *studentereksamener*. In a four-year program of course work and practice teaching, the students prepare to teach all classes in many subjects, one of which must be in a specialized field of education. They receive teaching certificates upon completion of the course. University degrees are given only at Denmark's *Laererhøjskole* (College of Education) or at the universities, where further training may be had in specialized subjects leading to a bachelor's or an advanced degree. Teachers in the academic-oriented *gym-*

nasium are required to have a university degree.

Although a special directorate heads the administration of the primary school and the teachers' colleges under the Ministry of Education, control of the elementary schools is actually in the hands of local school boards, composed for the most part of parents. In fact, one of the most distinctive features of the Danish schools is the influence parents have had on the educational program of the local school system. This has been especially true since 1970, when the Educational Supervision Act gave parents additional responsibility as members of the school board. In every school district, a local council sets up a school board and appoints one member. The remainder are elected by the parents of the school. In this way the parents, who are in the majority, have a great deal of influence in shaping the school's program. The decisions are theirs to make—as long as they are not in conflict with the basic policies set forth by the Ministry of Education.

The *gymnasium* is equivalent to an advanced high school or junior college, with a curriculum designed to prepare young people for further study at the universities and technical colleges. Only about 25 percent of students from the elementary school are admitted to the *gymnasium*.

The *gymnasium* (formerly the Latin school) has gone through several transformations since its establishment in the Middle Ages. The most recent change came in 1963, when a revision in the course divisions was made. Now the students in the *gymnasium* choose between two courses of study—the language course and the mathematics course, each one offering a choice of majors. In the language division, students may select the modern languages, the classical languages, civics and languages, or music. In the mathematics division, students may choose math and physics, civics and math, or the natural sciences.

After passing the *studentereksamen,* the student graduates from the *gymnasium* and qualifies for enrollment in a university or in any professional college or training institution. A delightful custom is the triumphant celebration that takes place when the students have succeeded in passing their *studentereksamener.* Wearing traditional red and white caps, they gather at such places as the square called Kongens Nytorv in Copenhagen and, joining hands, dance merrily around the famous equestrian statue of Christian V. Academic attainment is highly regarded in Denmark.

Numerous other educational opportunities are open to students who finish the ninth or tenth grade but do not go on to the *gymnasium.* For example, there are the "continuation schools" and the "youth schools," where students may get good preparation for various vocations. There is also the "higher preparatory course" (HF)—a two-year program of study leading to a diploma. From here, the student may seek admission to one of the teachers' colleges or, in some instances, to university classes. The "HF" courses are elective and have become extremely popular.

Under the Apprenticeship Act of 1956, any young man or woman over the age of sixteen may become an apprentice in some trade, provided the work period is supplemented by a period of training at technical schools. The contract period may be from two to four years in any of a hundred trades approved by the state. The apprentice is paid a salary and gets three weeks of paid vacation and up to three months of sick leave. Twenty-five to thirty thousand people are apprenticed each year in the different trades.

The kind of schools called *friskoler* (free schools)—designed on nonstructured principles—are becoming prevalent in Denmark. The oldest and probably most famous *friskole* is *Bernadotteskolen* in Copenhagen. This school, started after

World War II by Professor Carl Kragh-Muller, enrolls children from kindergarten through high school, although there are no grade levels as such and no set classes or examinations. Parents, teachers, and children cooperate in this informal learning situation, which provides many kinds of activities for developing the individual abilities of the child when he or she is ready and motivated.

Reforms in the schools have come about, not only through efforts of the administration but also through demands of the parents and the pressure of the students. A popular story in Danish educational circles goes like this:

Breakfast was ready. Mother Jensen went in to call Carl, fearing he would be late for school. "I don't want to go to school today," he moaned. "The teachers don't like me; the students don't like me. I feel like a failure. I can't seem to do anything right. Please, can't I stay home?"

"No, Carl dear, you really must go. The Directorate will not like it if you skip school. After all, you *are* the *Rektor* of the university."

At the present time, the position of *rektor* (vice-chancellor) of the University of Copenhagen is no easy job. The expanded student population demanding administrative and curricular reforms places enormous stress upon the governing body of the university.

Founded by Christian I in 1479, the University of Copenhagen has grown to be one of the most outstanding learning institutions in Europe. Supported entirely by the state and by private endowments, it is available to all students who have passed the *studentereksamener* and to qualified foreign students. The current enrollment of more than thirty-seven thousand students presents both space and curriculum problems. Overcrowded conditions, for instance, prevent the admission of foreign students to the medical college.

The University of Århus, founded in 1928 with only sixty-four students, has grown rapidly, until now it enrolls more than ten thousand students in five different faculties of learning on the expansive University Park campus in Århus.

Under the University Governance Act of 1970, the structure of the governing bodies of the universities was radically changed as the result of student demands. The act provided that professorial rule of internal affairs of the schools be abolished and that a third of the council seats be held by students. All governing councils—the Course Council, the Departmental Council, and the Chancellor's Council (the unhappy *Rektor*'s)—now contain a goodly proportion of university students.

Other Danish universities are attracting students by more experimental programs of study in what are called "university centers," like Odense University Center (founded in 1966), Roskilde University Center (1973), and Ålborg University Center (1974). Although each center offers traditional studies, a student may also take nonacademic courses worked out informally with an instructor. The newer university centers—corresponding somewhat to our two-year community colleges— have eliminated more traditional methods in an effort to provide a wider range of opportunities adapted to individual needs.

Recently, another kind of educational center has been established just north of the Limfjord in Jutland. Nordenfjord World University is a cluster of small, informal learning centers founded by students and teachers, whose concepts are similar to those of the new experimental college. Each center is an independent unit, financially as well as structurally. Each one specializes in a certain area—such as creative writing, arts and crafts, ecology, or visual arts—but all units assemble twice a month to present progress reports and participate in a seminar.

This kind of educational experience probably took a cue from the unique and popular folk high school, which had its origin in Denmark in the nineteenth century. Founder of this innovative kind of boarding school for adults was theologian N.F.S. Grundtvig. Grundtvig was opposed to the classical learning of the Latin school and felt that young people should also learn about existing social and political conditions. For this reason, he advocated the establishment of "pleasant boarding schools where youth and adults might study the national and civic life as all can and must share."

Grundtvig opened the first folk high school in 1844, in Rødding in southern Jutland. Seven years later, Kristen Kold, with Grundtvig's help, founded one at Ryslinge that was to become the pattern for many subsequent folk high schools both in Denmark and abroad.

At first, only people from the rural areas enrolled in the folk high schools. In a plain, *hyggelig* atmosphere young men and women lived, studied, and played together, inspired by lectures and discussions on timely issues, such as the agricultural cooperatives and political democracy. At the outset, the emphasis was on Danish life, literature, and social concerns, with no regimen of requirements, examinations, or credits.

Today there are more than eighty folk high schools in Denmark, all offering a variety of courses that provide good background for vocational study with full accreditation. They are attended by all classes of young people, mostly in the nineteen to thirty age bracket. The regular sessions vary from three to ten months, but short-term summer courses are also available. More than eighty-five hundred students enroll yearly, 15 percent from other Scandinavian countries.

The concept of the Danish folk high school spread to all parts of the world—even to India, China, and Japan. Immigrants brought the idea to the United States and established numerous similar schools.

Educational opportunities in Denmark are almost endless. Besides the generalized schools, there are any number of preparatory schools that provide training and retraining for persons of all ages and background. Evening classes and adult education courses attract those senior citizens whose long years in the school of life qualify them for "mod" courses and for classes geared to their interests. Through the Retraining Act of 1969, even the unskilled worker is now able to receive special training for a particular job or to improve his or her present craft or trade. The instruction is excellent, too. Incidentally, from the consumer's point of view, it's great to take your car into a Danish garage and actually have an expertly trained auto mechanic discover *immediately* why your radiator heats up!

Denmark will continue to make reforms in its educational program at a rapid rate, for the country has two characteristics that affect the nation's progress in every field: a keen and early appraisal of a problem and an inventiveness in solving the problem. The serious concern over school dropouts, for instance, led immediately to the hiring of more school psychologists and to legislation of free-time activities for youth—two steps that have already lessened the dropout rate and decreased the crime rate among young people. The attention and support Denmark has consistently given to its educational system have contributed greatly to the development of its strong economy and stable social structure.

Traditional Danish Christmas tree decorations

CHAPTER 11

CUSTOMS AND HOLIDAYS

HOW DO THE DANES derive so much fun out of their daily living—from the simple pleasures of life? Well, the Danes don't really need special forms of amusement, for they enjoy one another in the celebration of their various customs and holidays and in the sociability of eating and drinking.

A birthday is always a good excuse for a *fest* (celebration), particularly the fiftieth birthday, which is the one significant milestone for the Danes, giving a person the distinction of having lived for half a century. On their fiftieth birthday Danes are honored at their place of employment, by their boss and co-workers, by friends, relatives, and neighbors— all of whom join in the festivities of the auspicious occasion by bringing elaborate gifts and offering toasts to the honored guest. On every round-numbered birthday thereafter (sixty, seventy, and so forth), a Dane is also feted and his or her age publicized in the newspaper. When a person reaches the age of one hundred, the queen sends congratulatory wishes— not an infrequent occurrence, since Danes are long-lived, even in the United States, a fact attesting to their Viking vigor.

Every home has a flag, *Dannebrog,* which is raised on the birthday of any family member and flown on many other special occasions as well—Sundays, homecomings, visitations of honored guests, anniversaries, and, of course, legal holidays and church holidays. You will always see plenty of flags in Denmark. There are so many good reasons for displaying them!

The Queen's birthday, April 16, is an important day, when everyone wears a flag, and special ceremonies are held in Amalienborg Square. Prince Frederik, the heir apparent (born May 26, 1968), is usually feted at Fredensborg Castle, the royal summer residence. At these events, the Danish Royal Guard performs before the monarch's family and the viewing crowds, and then plays the American song, "Happy Birthday to You."

Weddings, anniversaries, baptisms, and confirmation ceremonies are also festive occasions, and many Danes still observe the customs pertaining to them.

Civil weddings are becoming more common in Denmark, a larger percentage in Copenhagen and other cities (40 percent) than in the towns and rural areas (27 percent). Before a couple can be married in the church, "bans" are announced by the pastor at three successive Sunday services prior to the ceremony.

The traditional wedding cake, *kransekage,* consists of layers of marzipan wreaths of diminishing size toward the top. Pieces of this festive cake are served to the wedding guests and are also sent to all persons who have sent gifts or good wishes to the couple. As is customary in many places, this sample is meant to be saved, not eaten. (A piece from Queen Victoria's wedding cake was auctioned at a sale in London in 1974—a bit dry, but extremely valuable!)

A sentimental bride may carry out another popular custom—that of placing her bridal bouquet upon the grave of Liden Kirsten at Vestervig Church in northwestern Jutland, the largest village church in Denmark. According to legend, Prince Buris (Henrikssen) was engaged to Kirsten, who was the half sister of King Valdemar I. The king violently opposed the marriage and mercilessly had the prince chained in prison. Liden Kirsten voluntarily joined her betrothed and stayed with him until both perished. Thereafter, it became the custom for a bride to place her bridal bouquet on Kirsten's grave in tribute to a woman's faithfulness and in pledge of her own.

Wedding anniversaries are also a good excuse for parties— the twenty-fifth, fiftieth, sixty-fifth, and seventy-fifth being the most important. But since these anniversaries are few and far between and sometimes unattainable, two new ones have been instigated to spark additional celebrations—the 12½-year and the 37½-year anniversaries to mark the copper and tin commemorative years, respectively! Anniversary plates with clever motifs (by Wiinblad) for every month of the year are favorite gifts for these occasions.

The festivities at anniversary parties consist of feasting, dancing, group singing, and giving of many gifts. Songs to familiar tunes are written to the feted couple, usually by a relative or close friend, and toasts and talks of tribute are given. At the restaurant or hotel dining room, where these events are commonly held, dancing follows the dinner, climaxed by an announcement from the orchestra leader: *"Nu spiller vi Brudevalsen!"* (Now we shall play the bridal waltz). At this time, the honored couple dances onto the floor, and the guests encircle them, holding hands. Singing the traditional song, the guests walk in and out toward the couple in the center until the song cues everyone to join in the general dancing.

The Danes often sing lustily as they dance to the old and new popular music. In fact, a merry gathering having a party in a dining hall may sound like a performing choral group. Danes openly enjoy group conviviality, seemingly unaware and unembarrassed by strangers or other guests who may be dining in the restaurant, for they are free to join in if they wish. And they often do.

In modern times, the christening of a child in church may provide some surprising contrasts. The baby is today—as of old—fancily dressed in a ruffly, laced, yard-long dress, which may practically cover the casual outfit of the mother in long pants or seem a bit too formal compared to the father's work attire. Young people, who may be opposed to the traditional for themselves, appear to preserve it for their children.

Confirmation has become more of a custom than a meaningful profession of faith. Yet, the prospect of the festive observance for the thirteen- and fourteen-year-olds—especially the gifts and attention they receive—is likely to prolong this Lutheran practice for some time to come.

Another cherished custom is that every boy and girl in the primary school in Denmark must make at least one "pilgrimage" to the top of *Himmelbjerget,* often with the rest of the class, for the purpose of attaining a particular cane, sold only there, to be kept as a permanent souvenir and evidence of an expedition to "Heaven's Mountain." That day is certainly a holiday for children.

It is important to mention that every weekend is a holiday in Denmark. Promptly at noon on Saturdays, all shops, stores, banks, groceries, and *kiosks* are closed for the weekend, and woe be it, if you have forgotten to purchase milk or bread for breakfast! Many restaurants are also shut down, and streets are deserted; the Danes are on their legalized weekend holiday.

The many holiday customs in Denmark are of unusual charm. As mentioned before, the Danish flag is a symbol of a tribute, and, proud of the land it represents, the Danes

exhibit it often and impressively. The flag is customarily
flown on all the following days:

January 1	New Year's Day
April 9	Occupation Day (at half-mast)
April 16	Queen Margrethe's birthday
April 26	Princess Caroline-Mathilde's birthday
May 5	Liberation Day
	Good Friday (half-mast)
	Easter Sunday
	Ascension Day
	Whit Monday
	Pentecost (Sunday and Monday)
	Store Bededag (Day of Prayer) fourth Friday after Easter
May 26	Crown Prince Frederik's birthday
June 5	Constitution Day
June 15	*Dannebrog*, Flag Day and Valdemar's Day
July 27	Prince Knud's birthday
October 24	United Nations Day
December 25	Christmas Day

Celebrations are also held on *Mortensdag,* early in November; *Fastelavn's Dag* (the day before Ash Wednesday);
and *Sankt Hans Dag,* June 23 (Midsummer's Eve).

The most significant and most celebrated occasion is, of
course, Christmas—a truly festive season in Denmark. More
delightful customs are observed at Christmas time in Scandinavia than, perhaps, in any other part of the world. Prep-
arations for the holidays are made weeks in advance, beginning with a rush to the stores to buy candles of all sizes and
colors before the first day of Advent—candles that will be
placed in original, handmade Advent wreaths and in the
windows of nearly every home.

Pynt is a meaningful Danish word for "decoration." It includes all the artful arrangements, objects, and trimmings for the house and Christmas trees, most of which are made by the various members of the family—a project that is anticipated the entire year.

Hearts have become the theme motif of a Danish Christmas—hearts for the Christmas tree, hearts for mobiles, and hearts for table decorations, all imparting the feeling that a Danish Christmas is from the heart.

A typical practice at Christmas time is the feeding of the birds. Every family places a sheaf of grain on a pole or on the gable of the barn for the birds' Christmas. The Danes protect and love their birds and will especially want you to hear the nightingale sing on a warm summer night.

The Christmas month begins on December 1, when children open their first Christmas token at 7:00 P.M. Every day thereafter they open a package until Christmas Eve, when the last—and most anticipated gift—is opened.

Baking for the holidays goes on for weeks. It includes such Danish specialties as *klejner, Julekage,* marzipan tarts, vanilla wreaths, *brune kager,* and *pebernøder.* Red cabbage, a "must" that is served with the traditional roast goose for Christmas dinner, may be prepared several days in advance, and *leverpostej,* a liver paste that is delicious on pumpernickel bread for breakfast on Christmas morning, is also made ahead of time.

The diminutive *Julenisse,* similar to Santa Claus except in size, is given a bowl of rice and milk on Christmas Eve. Set outside, it is gratefully eaten (by the family cat?) before morning.

Everyone goes to church on Christmas Eve. Services are held at 4:00 P.M. to allow time for preparation of the Christmas dinner when the family gets home. Mother places an almond in the rice pudding, and lucky is the one who finds it in his or her portion!

Father usually cuts the Christmas tree in the woods weeks previously. And before the tree is seen by the children, adults of the household decorate it with handmade ornaments of paper and felt—angels, birds, apples, hearts, and *nisser* (Christmas elves)—plus real candles, lighted before the children enter the living room, the youngest leading the way. The family and relatives join hands and circle the tree in the center of the room, singing at least *ten* of the traditional Christmas songs. (When, as young children, the authors of this book sang *"Nu har vi Jul igen,"* the first line of a famous carol, they thought it sounded like "New Happy Hooligan" and sang it loudly that way!) The second line of that song, *"Og Julen varer lige til Påske"* (And Christmas lasts until Easter), is not as true now as formerly, since the International Trade Fair meets in Denmark shortly after Christmas, and decorations must come down for this event.

Only after the musical interlude of singing are the gifts exchanged and opened. This is joyous Christmas Eve in Denmark.

The Christmas lottery is a common method used in Denmark for providing Christmas supplies and packages for the disadvantaged of the population. Sponsored by large daily newspapers, the contest offers numerous fabulous prizes to the lucky ticket holders, still allowing a sizable sum to be allotted to the yearly philanthropic project.

Fastelavn's Dag (the day before the fasting days of Lent) has its origin in the ancient belief that by exterminating cats, evil will be driven away. Hence an expression, *"Slå katten a' tønden"* (Strike the cat off the barrel) is occasionally put into practice on Fastelavn's Eve. More generally, the occasion calls for dressing up in costumes and masks, as Ameri-

can children do on Halloween, visiting friends and neighbors
and chanting:

> *Fastelavn er mit navn,*
> *Boller vil vi have;*
> *Hvis vi ingen boller får*
> *Så laver vi ballade.*

> My name is Lenten Eve;
> Sweet rolls I beg of you.
> If no sweet rolls I receive,
> I'll raise a hullabaloo!

If the visitors are identified, they must pay with rolls
instead!

At Pentecost *(Pinse),* not only is Sunday a special holy
day, but Monday—second day of Pentecost—is as well.
Church services are held on both days, providing a three-day
holiday.

On Constitution Day, June 5, Denmark observed in 1974
one hundred years of constitutional monarchy. June 5 is
traditionally a day for picnics, political speeches, and family
gatherings.

The celebration of Saint Hans's night on Midsummer Eve,
June 23, is an all-night fest anticipated by adults as well as
children. Friends and neighbors gather during the evening
after a large bonfire has been laid, preferably on the top of
a hill. The tradition signifies the burning of witches, who
have been the cause of all evil.

The Danes themselves can't tell you exactly why or how
the witches are burned—only that it is a lot of fun to join
hands and march up the hill singing, *"Sankt Hanses Dans,
Sankt Hanses Dans . . . "* The celebration may include a
more serious aspect, too. After the fire has been lighted,
there is a program of more singing and an inspirational

speech or two. In a talk given on St. Hans's Eve in June 1974, one dignitary said, "From this hilltop we can view the seasons of the year as they change the colors of the landscape, and we rejoice in our land. And although bitterness may at times overshadow our joy, we as a nation have been blessed with substantial material possessions. We belong to that part of the world where riches can be shared, while those in the Third World have only their poverty to share. Long live Denmark!" The program is followed by feasting and jollity the rest of the night.

Mortensdag, a November holiday, originally commemorated Martin Luther. It is a day of thanks, resembling the American Thanksgiving, except that the Danes eat goose instead of turkey at dinner that day.

Store Bededag (Long Day of Prayer), the fourth Friday after Easter, was established by Christian VI as the day when all persons in Denmark should unite in prayer. Before that time, there were approximately seven days of prayer to be celebrated at different times during the year. "Too many!" said the king, and he proclaimed one long day of prayer instead.

Many traditions can still be observed in every section of Denmark. One of these customs is that of placing a fir tree on the top of a building when the framework has been completed. Another quaint and solemn ritual takes place at Ebeltoft and Ribe. A watchman of the night still calls the hours and chants the words of the traditional "Song of the Watchman." The third stanza, translated by Bishop Kingo, goes thus:

> Master, maid, and boy, would you the hour know?
> It is time that you to rest should go.
> Trust in the Lord with faith, and careful be
> Of fire and light, for ten o'clock has struck.

The dinner party ritual of the **skål**

CHAPTER 12

FOOD AND HOSPITALITY

DRIVE-IN HAMBURGER STANDS do not exist in Denmark, possibly because dining is supposed to be a *hyggelig* and friendly occasion in appropriate, cheerful surroundings.

Although the daily fare in a Danish home is not the elaborate divertissement of cuisine found in the best restaurants and inns, most Danish meals and foods are different from American fare, as you might expect. Home-cooked food, though plain and thrifty, includes the typically Danish dishes, always nicely garnished and served. But if a guest is coming for dinner—that is a different story! The whole gamut of Danish specialties is lavishly prepared for a five-course banquet that would please a king, and they are served elegantly on a table decorated in artist's fashion, for every girl is taught in school and at home how to set a beautiful table. With great imagination and skill, the hostess arranges the tall tapers, lovely flowers, flags, nosegay napkins, blue-and-white porcelain china—adding, perhaps, a dainty figurine or two to form a harmonious setting for the feast. The silver, linens, furniture, and accessories—all of simple, modern Danish design—add beauty and dignity to the scene.

The Danes eat six times a day if you count morning and afternoon coffee and the snack before bedtime—a custom the Americans seem to be emulating now. Breakfast *(morgenmad)* is the most unvaried of the meals. You become accustomed to the assortment of breads—French, rye, and pumpernickel—the flavorful cheeses, plenty of butter and marmalade, and, naturally, several kinds of Danish pastry. A boiled egg, served in an egg cup and covered with a cozy, costs extra in a restaurant, but you can be sure it will be fresh. Certainly you must try a dish of pumpernickel crumbs, layered with yogurt and brown sugar—a delicious breakfast dish.

Lunch consists of *smørrebrød* (open-faced sandwiches) and beer. And don't pass lightly over those sandwiches. If you haven't tasted at least a dozen kinds of Danish sandwiches while visiting Denmark, you haven't lived. At the Oskar Davidsen restaurant on Åboulevard in Copenhagen, you may choose from 178 varieties, listed on a forty-eight-inch menu. The chef will even prepare all of them for you if you so desire; the experiment has been tried—several times— by doubting tourists!

The famous restaurant was first established in the 1880s. As a wine merchant, Oskar Davidsen made so many good wines that his shop was frequented by visitors from near and far. His wife, Petrea, decided to furnish tasty sandwiches to satisfy the appetites of the hungry customers, and thus began the House of Davidsen, famous sandwich restaurant. Today Oskar and Petrea's great-granddaughter and her husband, Adam Siesbye, are the operators. They also serve a number of delectable desserts, such as crisp pancakes topped with whipped cream and strawberries or wrapped around vanilla ice cream.

By the way, the Danes laugh when told that Americans eat pancakes for breakfast. These treats are definitely a dessert in Denmark, and delightfully tempting they are when embellished with gobs of whipped cream.

The intriguing sandwiches are the true connoisseur's concoction of numerous delicacies laid on tasty breads and artfully arranged. Try one, such as eel with scrambled egg, spinach, and fried mushrooms; or tomato, boned anchovies in oyster sauce, scrambled egg and chopped chives, on toast; or freshly smoked herring, egg yolk and chopped radishes; or liverpaste with grated beets; or mounds of tiny shrimp held together with curried mayonnaise and topped with parboiled egg.

In order to get the most out of a trip to Denmark, one must not only see the country—but taste it. An American doctor and his wife, who were visiting Denmark, planned to do just that, and they reminded their children to be sure to eat any of the different foods offered in this foreign country. To be on the safe side, the children ordered hamburgers, while the parents, being more adventuresome, ordered *boeuff tartare,* one of the sandwich specialties in Denmark. The admonishment backfired, as the curious couple was quite unprepared for the dish set before them—a generous heap of raw, scraped beef topped with a fresh, raw egg and a sprinkling of chives. The children eyed them daringly as the parents, in exemplary and courageous fashion and without *too* much hesitation, plunged into eating this most popular Danish sandwich.

Incidentally, *koldt bord* is the Danish term for the Swedish *smørgåsbord*. This service consists of a tiered table filled with many varieties of "cold" dishes—assortments of fish, meat, cheese, salads, breads, pickles, etc.—accompanied by *akvavit* and beer.

Danish sandwiches are always open faced and are eaten with a knife and fork, never picked up and eaten by hand. Americans in Denmark are identified immediately by the way they hold their fork—in the right hand instead of the left. Europeans don't shift the fork from the left to the right hand after cutting their food. If you understand Danish, you may hear a native say, "He's an American. See how awkwardly he eats!"

A Danish *middag* (evening meal) is a form of entertainment—enticing, exciting, and completely satisfying; several hours are spent in consuming this repast. As the main meal of the day, it begins and ends with talk and laughter. The first course of soup may be a choice of asparagus or mushroom soup, or perhaps *klar suppe*—a delicious, clear soup with carrot bits and thimble-size dumplings and meat balls (twenty or more in a first helping). The fish starter is usually an assortment of herring (sherry-marinated or pickled) served with miniature french bread. Or you may wish to start with canapés or delicate hors d'oeuvres of tiny shrimp, caviar, and liver paste.

The second course comes on a platter, always kept burning hot, and all eyes gaze upon it in appreciative anticipation, appraising the various dishes in connoisseur fashion. On the platter are the main meat courses of pork, beef tenderloin, or veal (fish might be plaice, trout, or cod), decorated with a gravy or sauce, bacon, parsley, bits of pickled beet, and garnished with green pepper, lemon, or orange slices—truly a work of art. At one end of the platter are potatoes—Danes love potatoes—french fries, chips, and *brunede kartofler,* a Danish specialty in which potatoes are browned in butter and sugar. Red cabbage, as common as our tossed salad, and green—yes, green—fresh, untarnished beans, add contrast of color to the plate, which is finally enhanced by the customary sliced, marinated fresh cucumber slices and flowers of lettuce and tomato (the latter meant for ornament only).

The waitress, or hostess, serves the first helping and sets an enormous bowl of brown gravy on the table. Danes take only small helpings of food on their plates at first, for they know they have a second, third, and fourth c

The dessert, which might be *rød grød* (red
Danish layer cake, or apple cake—all covere
cream—may add calories to the diet, but they
crown to the feast. The consumption of such a repast takes
some time, for it must be enjoyed with conversation and
wine.

Among other typically Danish dishes, to mention only a
few, are *sød suppe* (sweet soup, made with fruit), *aebleskiver*
(Danish pancake balls), *frikadeller* (Danish meat balls),
sildesalat (herring salad), *risengrød* (rice porridge), *rabar-
bergrød* (rhubarb pudding), *rullepølse* (spiced, pressed
veal), *medisterpølse* (pork sausage), and *romfromage* (rum
pudding). Of course, the genuine Danish pastry and desserts
are usually very rich—ranging from the almond-filled
kringler (coffee cake) to the raspberry-filled Napoleon cake.

Of wines, the Danes prefer the French red wine and their
own Cherry Heering, made in the eighteenth-century factory
in Christianshavn. The potent *akvavit* is the favorite Danish
snaps. It accompanies *smørrebrød,* especially pumpernickel
with fish, and is washed down with a glass of beer.

The familiar term, *skål,* is used when the wine glass is
raised in a toast to another person. The host will pick up his
glass first and say, *"Skål!"* as he looks directly into the eyes
of his guest, then sips a bit of wine, and looks again into his
or her eyes. The good host will *skål* each guest in turn; hus-
bands *skål* their wives, even when dining alone; and if
women are dining together, they will *skål* each other. But a
guest does not *skål* his hostess. Another tip—each time any
guest picks up his glass, the host, as well as everyone else at
the table, raises his glass and says, *"Skål!"*

Often the toast is in the form of a traditional lyric, sung
loudly and long to honor a guest. Everyone joins in singing,

"Han skal leve . . ." (Long may he live . . .) or, at least, comes in on the chorus, "Bravo, bravissimo."

And shame on those who refuse to bestow
A toast to . . . . whom we all know.

The *skål* is a gracious and pleasant custom.

But you do not *skål* with beer. Of course, beer is the national drink, and since the different kinds of beer have a varying amount of alcoholic content, you can choose according to your own taste. Both Carlsberg and Tuborg brew both light and dark beer; "pilsner" is light in color and in alcoholic content. Some 800 million bottles of beer are brewed annually by these two companies—an average of 137 pints of beer a year per person. However, no one who is driving drinks a second glass of beer, as he or she is punished severely if found to have consumed a drop above the legal limit.

Obviously, one of the national customs of Denmark is eating and drinking. And the Danes know a good thing when they taste it! They are all excellent cooks. Here are a few recipes for some of the most famous Danish dishes:

Frikadeller *(Danish Meat Balls)*

2 lbs. ground beef
½ lb. ground pork sausage
1 egg, well beaten
1 medium-sized onion, grated
2 T. flour
½ C. sifted bread crumbs
1 t. salt
½ t. pepper
½ C. milk

Combine meat and bread crumbs, and then gradually add flour. Add egg, onion, and seasonings. Slowly add milk and mix thoroughly. Shape mixture with a tablespoon before dropping into heated frying pan containing melted butter or cooking oil. Turn until well browned. Make brown gravy (recipe below) in same pan and pour over frikadeller.

Brown Gravy

1 small onion, chopped
1 T. margarine
1 T. flour
1 C. potato water
1 can mushroom soup (optional)
Salt and pepper

Remove meat balls. Melt margarine in skillet. Add chopped onion and brown slowly, stirring to prevent scorching. Add flour and mix well. Slowly add potato water, a little at a time, stirring each time to make it smooth. Season to taste and simmer until thickened. Add mushroom soup, milk, or cream for creamier gravy.

Rødkål I *(Red Cabbage)*

1 medium-sized head of red cabbage
3 T. butter
4 T. sugar
¼ C. vinegar
¼ C. water
1 T. salt
¼ C. currant jelly

Quarter the cabbage and shred into long thin strips. Brown butter in heavy kettle, add shredded cabbage, and stir well. Then add salt, sugar, vinegar, and water. Cover and simmer slowly over low heat for several hours. When cabbage is tender, add currant jelly and stir until it is dissolved. Red cabbage tastes best if it has been made the day before and reheated.

Rødkål II

1 medium-sized head of red cabbage
3 T. butter
½ C. brown sugar
¼ C. vinegar
1 C. water
1 T. salt

Quarter the cabbage and shred into long thin strips. Melt butter in heavy kettle, add shredded cabbage, and stir well. Then add salt, brown sugar, and water. Cover and simmer for an hour or until cabbage is crisply tender. Drain. Add vinegar, mix well, and simmer, covered, for 10 minutes longer, until red coloring is restored.

Sildesalat *(Herring Salad)*

2 or 3 medium salt herring or 5 oz. jar of herring
1 C. boiled diced potatoes
1 C. diced pickled beets
1 C. cooked veal, finely chopped
1 C. apples, peeled and finely diced
1 medium onion, chopped
1 T. sugar
1 T. vinegar or ¼ C. chopped pickles

Soak herring overnight in cold water. Drain. Remove bones and skin and cut into cubes. Mix with chopped potatoes, beets, veal, apples, onion, sugar, and vinegar. Mix with vinegar dressing (recipe below) and season to taste. Serve.

Vinegar Dressing

2 eggs
½ t. mustard
2 T. vinegar
1 T. sugar
½ t. salt

Whip eggs slightly and stir in other ingredients. Heat slowly in saucepan, stirring constantly until it comes to a boil. Remove and let cool. Add to salad before serving. Garnish with hard-cooked eggs and pimiento strips.

Aebleskiver *(Danish Pancake Balls)*

5 eggs, separated
¾ C. milk, cream, or buttermilk
2 C. flour
2 t. baking powder
½ t. salt
½ t. soda
2 T. sugar
grated rind of 1 lemon
½ t. powdered cardamom

Beat egg yolks. Add milk, sugar, salt, cardamom, and lemon rind. Sift flour, soda, and baking powder together and add to egg mixture. Beat egg whites until stiff and add last. Place a tablespoon of shortening in each cup of the aebleskiver pan. When pan is hot, pour in about two tablespoons of batter into each cup. Turn quickly with knitting needle or poultry fastener as soon as edges are bubbly. Turn ball frequently to prevent burning. Serve with jam, powdered sugar, or syrup.

Klejner *(Danish Fry-cakes)*

3 eggs
½ C. butter
1 C. sugar
½ t. salt
1 t. baking powder
¼ C. cream
1 t. cardamom seed (crushed)
3½ C. sifted flour

Cream butter and sugar until soft, and then stir in eggs and cream. Sift flour, baking powder, and spices together, and add to mixture. Roll out to ⅛-inch thickness, and cut with pastry wheel into 1-inch strips. Cut again diagonally cross-wise into 3-inch lengths. Make a slit in the center, and pull one end through slit carefully. Cook in deep fat until light brown, turning and removing quickly with knitting needle or long pronged fork. Drain on paper towel.

Aeblekage *(Danish Apple Cake)*

3 C. dry bread crumbs
4 T. sugar
¼ C. butter
¾ C. sweetened applesauce
1 C. red raspberry jam
½ pt. whipping cream

Melt butter in heavy skillet. Add sugar and crumbs and mix over low heat until lightly browned. Place a layer of crumbs in shallow baking dish or a mold, lightly buttered. Add alternate layers of applesauce and crumbs, with one layer of red raspberry jam in between. Top layer should be crumbs. Press well, and bake in 350-degree oven for 30 minutes. Unmold on a serving dish, and top with whipped cream.

Romfromage *(Rum Pudding)*

3 T. gelatin
1 C. cold water
5 egg yolks
3 egg whites
¼ C. rum or 1 T. rum flavoring
2 C. milk
2 C. whipping cream
1 C. sugar
½ t. salt

Soften gelatin with cold water. Beat yolks of eggs with sugar and salt until creamy and lemon-colored. Add milk and cook slowly, stirring constantly until custard forms. Remove from heat immediately. Add the gelatin to the hot custard. Cool and add rum. Whip egg whites and cream separately. As mixture begins to thicken, fold in whipped cream and beaten egg whites. Refrigerate several hours before serving with a red fruit sauce.

The Tivoli Gardens in Copenhagen

CHAPTER 13

RECREATION AND SPORTS

THE DANISH PEOPLE take their recreation seriously. They believe fervently that *recreation* is what the word means—a rejuvenation of mind, body, and spirit through relaxation, play, and exercise. Health is of such prime importance to the people of Denmark that laws enforce vacations. A portion of every person's salary is withheld for vacation expense and must be used for no other purpose. The philosophy behind this idea is that the health of employees is related to the amount and quality of their production. Consequently, between May and September each year, all the Danes plan a four-week *ferie* (vacation), anticipating how they can spend their merited recreation pay most profitably.

With the coming of the first warm spring days, the Danes begin to take their leave of cities and towns and head for the beaches, parks, and summer cottages—or for more distant resorts in other countries, such as Germany, Switzerland, Spain, Italy, Majorca, or the Canary Islands—to soak up some of the sun's rays.

More than half the people in Denmark own a summer cottage, or *sommerhus*— not just the rich, for having a cottage is not associated with class or rank. Some years ago, land was cheap, and the skillful Dane, taught to work with tools, would build a small cabin in some idyllic spot near lake, forest, or beach. Now thousands of these summer cottages dot the coastal and island areas, on heathland, hills, or in wooded hideaways—healthful retreats from the workaday world.

For those who do not own a summer house, such a house may be rented through organizations like *Dansk Folkeferie,* a Danish vacation bureau that rents out seacoast and garden houses to the public at prices ranging from fifteen to one hundred dollars a week. Application is by lottery (drawing of a low number), and competition is great.

Of course, outdoor activities occupy many of those awaited leisure hours. Nearly every youngster learns swimming almost as early as walking, while sailing and boating are favorite water sports. For anglers, the lakes, streams, and ocean are practically at their back door and stocked with all types of fish.

Camping is becoming an extremely popular outdoor activity for persons of all ages. Numerous camping sites are found all over Denmark and are clearly marked with a flag and the single word *camping.* Colorful tents and trailers are seen in increasing numbers at these scenic, accessible areas, well-equipped with convenient facilities.

Hiking is one of the most exhilarating of the sports the Danes pursue. You might say they walk energetically to work up (or work off) an appetite, as a Danish meal is not exactly prepared for weight watchers! The inexpensive and healthful sport of hiking offers many opportunities for young and old to see the country, and the country offers many opportunities for the hiker. A popular family pastime is to follow one of the many marked trails in the lovely national parks laid out by the Tourist Association of Denmark.

One of the most frequented walks is called "The Walking Tour" in the Marselisborg Woods south of Århus. It is a tour of about seven kilometers (under four and a half miles) from Ørnereden, a restaurant whose name is derived from a couple of white-tailed eagles who nested there, to Skovmølle —another restaurant situated at a three-hundred-year-old mill that still grinds grain. At short intervals, the route is marked with bright yellow spots of paint on the tree trunks. A detailed map of the park, showing the paths that wind through these enchanting surroundings, is available for wanderers to test their familiarity with nature's best exhibits.

Nature study paths of this sort were originally planned in 1929 by A. E. Skjøt-Petersen, a biology teacher at Marselisborg Grammar School in Århus. Tags with explanatory texts about the trees and suggestions for studying the ways of the hare, pheasant, or squirrel or watching the growth of ice crystals in the pond were attached to trunks of trees. To this day, hundreds of such tags provide seasonal interest and challenge to entire families for making innumerable botanical and biological discoveries in the great out-of-doors.

Strolling on the majestic cliffs or along the beach on the island of Møn is another enjoyable experience. Different routes have been carefully planned here for both the tenderfoot and the more energetic hiker, to provide a view of the picturesque cliffs, coastline, and distant islands.

Less than twenty miles north of Copenhagen, near Klampenborg, lies the inviting *Dyrehaven* (Deer Park), originally the private hunting grounds of Christian V. Now it provides miles of lovely walks among the beeches and oaks for the enjoyment of the public the year round, with the exception of one day when it is reserved for the use of the royal family.

Several unusual outdoor museums attract many summer vacationers and foreign tourists as well. The best known of these is in Århus—*Den Gamle By* (The Old Town), a reconstructed village, as quaint and realistic as in the olden days. Fifty Danish houses and specialty shops, cobbled

streets, and a water mill tell the story of Danish life a century
ago. The old Elsinore Theater, built in 1817, is of special
pride. It is particularly attractive to visitors during the summer months, when excellent operas, concerts, and plays are
presented on its stage.

What child would not enjoy exploring and examining the
unusual structures built by early rural inhabitants of Denmark? Such a museum is located in a setting at *Frilandsmuseet* in northern Zealand, where a combination of many old
gaards portrays an earlier society, and demonstrations such
as folk dancing, candle making, threshing, spinning, and flax
processing provide learning experiences for adults as well as
children.

At Hjerl Heath, in another outdoor museum on the far
western coast of Jutland—in an area of twenty-five hundred
acres of forest, fields, and meadow—typical farm buildings
have been reconstructed to demonstrate ways of life from
many eras—an attraction that welcomes nearly two hundred thousand visitors annually.

And what are some of the other holiday pleasures the
Danes enjoy?

"Flowers make people happy and bright of spirit." Such
is the motto of the magnificent flower park—the *Jesperhus
Blomsterpark*—covering approximately thirty acres of land
near the city of Nykøbing on the island of Mors in northern
Jutland. This wonderland of flowers and fantasy was started
in 1965. Paths of crushed mussel shells lead past garden
beds of every color and description, including thirty thousand
roses and hundreds of shrubs, cacti, and annual flowers. The
gardens, fountains, viewing towers, playgrounds, greenhouse,
aquarium, and solarium cafeteria are all combined into a
beautiful masterpiece of architectural landscaping. The
many red and white Danish flags, waving loftily, can be

seen from a great distance and attract thousands of Danes and tourists to a smiling holiday setting.

The Danes are fond of a carnival atmosphere, good restaurants, and theater. All of these are combined into the outstanding entertainment park of Denmark—Tivoli Park in Copenhagen. From May 1 till September 15, this fairytale garden in the center of the city is open to throngs of pleasure seekers—more than 200 million of whom have passed through its gates since it began operation in 1843. In this enchanting playground, you wander through tree-shaded lanes, beside fountained lakes edged with gorgeous flowers in season, past inviting amusement rides, booths, and arcades, to the outdoor pantomime theater, concert hall, and open-air variety theater, where international artists perform regularly.

Legoland (meaning "playland"), located near Billund in Jutland, is a mecca for children of all ages. This miniature town, covering several acres of ground, contains replicas of famous cathedrals, castles, manor houses, airports, space launches, harbors, ships, and houses—all built of the small finely wrought plastic bricks, called Lego blocks, that can be snapped together into the most ingenious creations. Legoland is a fanciful place, containing the things that dreams are made of.

In Denmark bicycling can hardly be called a sport—or even a pastime—since, like walking, it is a common means of locomotion for young and old alike, as well as a much-needed form of exercise. Even the red-coated mail carriers deliver the mail on bicycles. Because of the energy crisis, the bicycle has increased even more in popularity. Some day it may become the one and only means of travel on busy city streets. The bicycle is now a common and most welcomed gift on the occasion of a fiftieth birthday!

Some form of sport has been a recreational activity for

the majority of Danes for many years. Amateur athletics
began in Denmark with the establishment of the first rifle
clubs in the 1860s, clubs whose activities soon included
gymnastics. By 1890, other sports had become popular, and
clubs were formed for swimming, walking, weight lifting,
wrestling, football, rowing, and boxing.

In 1896, the Danish Sports Federation *(Dansk Idraets-
Forbund)* was founded—a federation of amateur sports organizations in Denmark, whose purpose is to promote interest in Danish amateur sports. Besides coordinating six thousand clubs and the forty-three organizations, of which the
Danish Football Association is the largest, the federation
sets up amateur regulations and provides financial help for
the individual groups. More than 1.3 million people are
enrolled and involved in the federation's athletic program
alone. Membership in the Danish Rifle, Athletics, and Gymnastics Association, and the Workmen's Sports Association
adds another seven hundred thousand members to a total of
more than 2 million sports participants—nearly one out of
every two persons in Denmark.

This overwhelming interest in sports may be due to the
fact that professionalism in sports has never been encouraged
in Denmark. The ideal has long been that all persons should
have opportunity for participating in leisure time athletics—
that to support the professional is to deprive the amateur.

"Sport for the Many and Sport for Many Years" is the
motto on the distinctive badge awarded annually by the
ruling monarch, who is the patron of the sports associations,
to the men and women who have passed various proficiency
tests. About eight hundred awards are presented each year.

There are two other major goals of the Danish Sports
Federation, the largest of the athletic associations in Denmark. They are to keep politics out of athletics and to pro-

mote the teaching of gymnastics in the public schools. Chairman Carl Larsen believes that physical education in the schools should continue to be obligatory or the physical vigor of Danish youth will degenerate.

Among outdoor competitive sports, the event with the greatest following and participation is association football, which is very similar to American soccer. The game is played by eleven people on a side, with one of them assigned as a goal tender or goalie. The purpose of ten of the players from the other side is to kick the ball past the goalie into the net. Hands must not be used. It is a great spectator sport, with a season from April until November. When the World Football Meet is in progress, travel is affected significantly; most people are at home, virtually glued to their television sets.

The football pool *(Dansk Tipstjeneste)* is the popular, legalized betting contest, in which you may purchase a card, mark out the teams you think will win, and deposit it with the cigar store dealer. If your choices are correct, you will win valuable prizes. Support for Danish sports comes chiefly from this source and from membership subscriptions, total sums of which amount to more than 15 million dollars annually. Substantial grants and loans are made to clubs and communities for athletic halls and facilities.

Excellent athletic buildings *(idraetshaller)* have been built in all areas of the country—more than two hundred and fifty in all. Nearly every town, even the smallest village, has one of these fabulous, eye-catching sports structures that now seem paramount in the civic planning of the Danish community.

Danish people have long been famous for their gymnastics, a sport which now has a separate organization, the Danish Gymnastics Federation. Gymnastic teams, directed by the famous Niels Bukh (1880-1950), became internationally known for their performances in many countries. In 1920, Bukh founded the first athletic school in Denmark. Located at Ollerup, it is one of the six athletic schools in the country today. Others are located in Gerlev, Vejle, Viborg, Sønderborg, and Århus.

Competitive sports started as early as 1887 with the Danish Rowing Club, and now include many more, such as yachting, skating, swimming, cycling, fencing, boxing, badminton, running, high jumping, and archery.

Denmark has been well represented at the Olympics since three Danes attended the first meet of modern times in Athens in 1896. In 1906, the first women to perform in an Olympic stadium were the Danish gymnastics team, the "princesses," so-called because they were invited to stay at the palace of the Danish-born King Georg I of Greece. The hospitality of the king was a gesture to demonstrate his respect for women, since their appearance in Athens at a public athletic event was quite unheard of at that time.

Because Denmark's sports are a leisure activity for the many instead of an honor for the few, this nation may not win as many Olympic "firsts," but it follows the motto that "The goal is not to win, but to compete with honor." Yet, Denmark has not done too badly. It has taken part in every modern Olympiad and has always succeeded in winning medals. By far the greatest number of gold and silver medals won by Denmark at the World Olympic Games have been in badminton, and the second greatest number have been in archery. Some of the other "firsts" Denmark has taken since 1896 have been in weight lifting, shooting, wrestling, rowing, diving, boxing, fencing, cycling, swimming, yachting, boating, and riding.

Whether in active sports or leisure activities during those highly treasured vacation periods, the Danes crave *morskab og selskab* (fun and fellowship) in their recreation. That is what they mean when they say, *"Ha' en god ferie!"* (Have a good vacation).

Folktales from Jutland:
Molboerne (the inhabitants of Mols), after P. Lundsgaard

CHAPTER 14

COURTESY AND HUMOR

A PROVERB THAT SAYS, "A happy face is the sign of a glad heart," truly applies to the Danish people. Strangers in Denmark see and feel immediately the cheerful and generous spirit that seems to be a Danish characteristic. The average Dane will go miles out of his or her way to extend a helping hand to a visitor, and perhaps that is the very reason for the Danes' happiness.

A pleasant *"god dag"* (good day) is spoken by everyone in greeting the butcher, the baker, the sales clerk, or persons on the street. In fact, when you have exchanged the greeting with all the people you have seen, you begin to feel you have made many acquaintances and friends.

"Tak, tak, tak" (Thanks, thanks, thanks) is also heard everywhere repeatedly, like a clock. Without exception, whether you buy a loaf of bread, a newspaper, or a bus ticket, you will hear, *"Tak for det"* (Thanks for that) upon paying for it, which makes you feel that you should at least have bought a Danish Christmas plate! And even when the clerk hands you your parcel, you hear, *"Vaer så god,"* which means, literally, "Be so kind" ("to accept" being understood).

"Vaer så god" is also spoken by the hostess when she invites you to come to dinner when it is ready. The English language has no proper equivalent for this invitation, except

"Dinner is ready." You will also be surprised when the beautician, the teller at the bank, or the bus driver says, *"Farvel!"* (Good-bye) when you leave. Again, you feel as though you have met—and left—another friend.

Completely unexpected is the response often given to your simple "thank you" to someone who has extended you a favor. *"Det var så lidt"* (It was such a little thing) is meant to express the willingness to apply the Golden Rule, and, accompanied by a pleasant inflection of the voice, it conveys a ring of kindness one does not anticipate. Such was the case when the writer asked the telephone operator to find a number for her, and upon thanking the woman, received the reply, "It was such a little thing!" How nice!

On the appropriate occasion, *"Tak for mad!"* (Thanks for the meal) is a Dane's instinctive response to the hostess when leaving the dinner table. And *"Jeg beder"* (I beg of you)—the equivalent of our "don't mention it"—may be the hostess's reply, or she may simply say, *"Velbekommen"* (You're welcome). Good Danes will also say, *"Velbekommen!"* whenever they see anyone eating heartily when they themselves are not partaking.

Whenever a guest meets a host or hostess again, shortly after being entertained in his or her home, he should never forget to say, *"Tak for sidst"* (Thanks for the last time) in appreciation of the hospitality. And upon leaving a person and hoping to see him or her again, one says, *"På gensyn"* (Till we meet again) after saying a cordial *"farvel."*

The Danes still use the polite form of "you" (*"de"*) to strangers and the more familiar *"du"* to friends and family, although the value of continuing this custom is being questioned today. "Please" is a must, but the expression in Danish, *"Vaer så venlig at. . ."* or *"Må jeg bede om. . ."* takes longer to say and calls for a little practice. On the other hand, "excuse me," used in appropriate situations, is a short and simple *"Undskyld."*

One should not have to be reminded to take along a bouquet of flowers for the hostess when invited to dinner, since flowers are plentiful and inexpensive in Denmark. A dozen roses may cost no more than a dollar, and a cyclamen plant seventy-five cents.

Shaking hands upon being introduced is not limited to the male sex. This gracious custom is always used when one meets someone or takes leave; to omit it would be considered rude. Even small children in school are taught this courtesy —the little boys bowing and the girls curtsying as they shake hands with visitors and often with their teacher at the end of the school day.

Used consistently and frequently by everyone, from the youngest to the oldest Dane, these small amenities of word and deed seem to reflect courteous consideration of one another and an appreciation of "the little things." Whether good manners are important to one or not, they do express sincere friendliness. That friendliness is an earmark of the Danes.

The Danish people are known for their good sense of humor. John Steinbeck said, "If I were a dictator, I would not occupy Denmark for fear of being laughed to death." In fact, the story is told that while Hitler's armies occupied Denmark during World War II, the Danes refused to have their laughter repressed. From a long list of numbered jokes, they would call out to one another simply a number *("Nummer tolv," "Nummer seks")* and go off into gales of hilarious laughter, leaving the uncomprehending German soldiers glaring and glum.

Danes seem always ready for a joke or at least a jovial greeting, and they respond to the simplest anecdote with resounding laughter. The jokes tend to be broad and a bit earthy at times, and the most obvious situation always seems the funniest.

A pun or a play on words sounds funnier, somehow, in Danish than in English translation! And saying the opposite of what is really true, although slapstick humor, always brings a laugh. The jesting Dane will probably say to a friend, "Lovely day, is it not?" as he slushes through a torrential rainstorm.

Nor do the Danes hesitate to laugh at themselves. Commonly heard everywhere are jokes about taxes, the prime minister, and the government.

The beloved illustrator and comedian Robert Storm Petersen, who died in 1949, is still regarded as the most gifted author of modern Danish humor. Throughout a generation, he did illustrations for the daily paper *Berlingske Tidende,* drew the comic strip "Peter and Ping," published jokes, cartoons, and illustrations for Sunday and foreign newspapers, and wrote many humorous stories and joke books—all under the signature "Storm P." As an actor in burlesques in cabarets, he won the hearts of a wide audience with his sparkling wit. A master of his art, Petersen worked painstakingly on his sketches, completing more than sixty thousand exceedingly witty illustrations. His imagination and his insight into human frailties equalled the quality of his fine drawings. His ideas were born from comical incidents, past and present, and they are as timely today as when they were first conceived. His delightful book of illustrated cartoons, entitled *Aktuelle,* was published in 1974. Here is a typical Storm P. joke:

"What are you thinking about?"

"I am thinking about whether it is possible not to think about anything."

Willy Andersen is another noted Danish sketcher; he died in 1973, shortly before the publication of his second volume of *Ser Man Det* (Seen in Fact). He illustrated hundreds of actual, yet curious, events that he gathered from wide sources. Known as the Danish counterpart to Ripley's *"Believe It or Not,"* Andersen's books are both entertaining and enlightening. For instance, you learn that even though electric lights on Christmas trees are becoming more common each year, the number of candles still being used on family Christmas trees in Denmark total about 25 million—the production of which is begun immediately after Christmas for the following year.

Of never-to-be-forgotten fame for humor is N. H. Volkesen, who was Pierrot in the Tivoli Pantomime Theater for fifty years. Originally an acrobat, he would bring tears of laughter from adults and children alike as he clowned with playful agility in the pantomime acts. "Pierrot, say something!" the children cried as the dumbshow ended, and Pierrot would lead them in a rousing round of *hurrahs*.

The buffoonery of this early comedian has been carried on by succeeding Pierrots. Adults are still convulsed with laughter, and children still scream loudly for a word from their comical hero at the end of the act. It is almost more fun to watch the delightful response of the Danes than it is to see the pantomime itself.

The most popular jokes are told on persons from other areas of the country. Best known, perhaps, are the Molbo stories, which have been handed down about the people in Mols—a section of eastern Jutland near Ebeltoft. These jokes are still told good-naturedly, though they are, of course, more legendary than real.

Once the Molboers were afraid the enemy would attack and capture all that was of value on Mols, especially their treasured church bell. Some of the clever townsmen decided to hide it from the enemy by sinking it into the sea. They placed the bell in a boat and rowed out in the Kattegat, where they dropped the bell over the side of the boat. Suddenly it occurred to them that, although the bell would be hidden from the enemy, it would also be lost to them. "The answer is simple," said one. "Just make a notch on the boat at the exact place we heaved the bell overboard, and only we will know what the notch means!" This they did and felt confident that they would be able to find the bell again.

Another familiar Molbo story is told of the rich man who was walking along the road and came to a poor man stretched out for a nap on the road. His feet, outstretched, were clad in old, worn-out shoes. The rich man, having bought a new pair of boots, felt sorry for the sleeping man and put the new boots on him, taking the old ones with him. Along came a man driving a large wagon, and he yelled at the sleeping one, "Take your feet out of the road, or I'll run over them!" Half waking up, the poor man looked at his feet and, seeing the handsome boots, said, "Go ahead, run over them. They aren't my feet."

The story called "The Light That Failed" relates how several men at an inn had their lamp blown out. They fumbled for matches to re-light it, but found only two. The man with one match dropped his. To find it, another man lit the second match, but they could not locate it, so he blew that match out. They were left in the dark!

The ability to make light of a serious situation has been a saving grace for the Danes. Times of crisis—the war, the depression, the high taxes, political revolt—have always supplied humorists and cartoonists with material for clever quips and caricatures, providing a welcome emotional release for the populace.

The energy crisis is definitely one timely subject that is made easier to bear by jokes and good-humored ridicule. Witness the cartoon showing the family sitting behind the television set to keep warm!

A Dane will often joke about his personal affliction or the hardships and frustrations of life. Piet Hein's grooks, mentioned earlier, are an example of this. Here is Hein's Consolation Grook:

CONSOLATION GROOK

Losing one glove
is certainly painful,
but nothing
    compared to the pain
of losing one,
throwing away the other,
and finding
    the first one again.

In proverbs and other sayings, Danish humor tends to point up the truth most graphically. *"Man skal gå på jorden, selv om den er gloende"* (One must walk on the earth, even if it be scorching). Freely translated is another famous maxim—"No harm done," which is funnier in Danish, *"Der er ingen ko på isen,"* or literally, "There is no cow on the ice."

Of course, the Danes are very proud of their famous humorist-entertainer, born in Jutland, Victor Borge, who is acclaimed in the United States as well as in Denmark. "My father should have been my grandfather, only he didn't know it!" quips Borge, recalling that his father, Bernhard Rosenbaum, was sixty-two years old when he was born.

As Borge Rosenbaum, Victor inherited the talent of his violinist father, who for thirty-three years played in the King's Chapel. His son was a child prodigy—recognized early for his talent. "I played the piano from the time I could tell black keys from white keys," says Borge. For seventeen years, he appeared as pianist in the Odd Fellow Palace. From the piano, he switched to the organ and performed in many and various concert halls, dance halls, and churches, chiefly in Copenhagen. Then he discovered his gift of playing and talking at the same time.

From a variety show in Ziegunerhallen, the comedian went to the Bellevuteatret in 1937, where he first introduced his "Phonetic Punctuation of a Sentence," which, given again in the theater at Århus in 1971—in Danish, of course—still brought uproarious laughter.

Borge left Denmark in 1940, after successfully performing in four films. He married his American-born wife on August 28 of that same year in New York. In the United States, he worked hard at learning the English language and was helped by such friends as Rudy Vallée and Bing Crosby, in whose shows his new career was begun.

The *New York Times* has called him "the world's funniest

man." Denmark still acclaims him as such, but also recognizes him as a great man. Through his philanthropic gestures of kindness as well as through his humor, he won, in 1954, the Schubert Medal, an award originating in Austria that is given every four years to an outstanding musical performer. The tribute bestowed upon him was this: "A good laugh also contributes to mankind's welfare." In a world where grimness is commonplace, that is no small contribution to make for more than a generation.

Explorers of the cosmos
Inserts: Astronomer Tycho Brahe
Physicist Niels Bohr

Chapter 15

FROM STARS TO ATOMS

RESEARCH BY DANISH SCIENTISTS has been devoted to the largest components of the universe—the stars—and the most minute components—electrons and protons. And scientists of Denmark have made definite contributions in all fields of endeavor from A to Z—from astronomy to zoology, in fact. This brief chapter can cite only a few luminaries.

Tycho Brahe, a Danish nobleman's son, set the pace for astronomy, and what a start that was! An eclipse of the sun in 1560 awakened in the young man a profound interest in astronomical science. He promptly gave up the study of law his family had envisioned for him and delved into the courses that led him to his fame as the first "modern" scientific astronomer.

On the night of November 11, 1572, Brahe noticed in the constellation Cassiopeia a brilliant new star, ten times brighter than the brightest star in the configuration. For a year and a half he studied it, making copious notes on its character and position until it finally disappeared from sight.

Brahe wrote up his observations in a scholarly treatise called *De Stella Nova* (The New Star), whose name alone would have brought the author fame, inasmuch as an exploding star of that type is still called a *nova*.

The study so impressed King Frederik II that he decided to give the young scientist an island called Hven, located in the sound between Sweden and Denmark, for the purpose of developing an astronomical observatory and a school for astronomers. Here at Uranienborg (named after the planet Uranus) Brahe labored for twenty-one years, measuring stars and planets and making numerous tables of the positions of the stars. Because of the excellence of his calculations and observations, scientists from all over Europe came to study at Uranienborg.

As an observer, Brahe was unsurpassed. In fact, it has been said that he was a master link in the chain of thinkers that led to modern-day understanding of the world and the universe: Brahe, Kepler, Copernicus, Galileo, Newton, Einstein. Tycho Brahe was a man of the Renaissance— astute, knowledgeable, and tremendously productive.

Following in the footsteps of this great scientist, some fifty years after his death, came Ole Roemer—astronomer, physicist, and engineer (1644-1710). As an engineer he is remembered as the man who planned the masterful waterworks and fountain at Versailles. But as a scientist, he is most famous for being the first person to measure the speed of light. Recently discovered notes have also shown that he invented the thermometer and knew how to measure the coefficient of expansion in metals.

The extensive work in the refraction of light by one of Roemer's contemporaries, Rasmus Bartholin, led in modern times to the invention of the Polaroid camera. This versatile scientist also discovered the Bartholin's glands in the female body.

The field of physics owes a great debt to Hans Christian Ørsted (1777-1851), who discovered electromagnetism. He observed that an electric current passing through a copper wire would create a magnetic field, causing a compass needle to deflect from pointing north. From that simple observation dates the word *oersted*—meaning a unit of magnetic intensity. From Ørsted's discovery have come the manifold uses of electromagnetism, including electric measuring instruments, electric power generators, electric motors, and so forth.

Danish scientists of the later nineteenth and early twentieth centuries have gained international reputations by pioneering in many fields. Four distinguished men have received Nobel Prizes in physiology and medicine: Niels Finsen in 1903 for his treatment of diseases with concentrated light rays; August Krogh in 1920 for his discovery of the system of action of blood capillaries; Johann Fibiger in 1926 for discovery of a parasite that causes cancer; and Henrik Dam in 1943, an outstanding biologist and university professor, for his discovery of vitamin K.

An illustrious Nobel Prize winner in physics (in 1922) was the world-famous scientist Niels Heinrich David Bohr (1885-1962), who is called the "father of the modern atom." The Bohr theory describes the structure of the atom and explains how atoms give off energy. Bohr proposed that electrons revolve in fixed orbits about a central nucleus, and that when an electron jumps from one orbit to another, energy is released.

Besides being a noted scientist, Bohr was also a great humanist. The story is told of his extemporaneous speech at a formal dinner party honoring a Swedish archbishop. When Niels Bohr was called on, everyone expected him to address his remarks to scientific theories and the atomic bomb. Instead, he spoke only on the subject of peace—an international peace that should evolve through a union of the scholars of all nations. The dinner host (and narrator of this incident) reported that Bohr's message made all the guests feel almost as if they had been at a church service.

Bohr spent most of his scientific career at the Institute for Theoretical Physics in Copenhagen. But he ordered all work stopped there in 1940, when the Nazis invaded Denmark. The dramatic flight this distinguished scientist later made from German-occupied Denmark in 1943 reads like a storybook thriller. Assisted by his associates and guards, he escaped at night by secret passage from Carlsberg through a certain gate, where he was met and rushed by car to the sound. Crawling on his hands and knees through tall grass and shrubs, he reached a rowboat on the coast and silently maneuvered his way through the water around the Nazi guardposts until he reached the shores of neutral Sweden.

After the war, Bohr stressed again the vital theme of peace efforts in his "Open Letter to the United Nations," expressing the idea that open efforts—especially now in light of the discovery of atomic power—constitute the greatest hope for world peace, that the free exchange of ideas among nations is essential to control the use of nuclear weapons and provide a solution to international problems.

Two other great honors were bestowed on Niels Bohr. In 1947, he became the first commoner to receive the Royal Danish Order of the Elephant for his meritorious service to Denmark. And in 1957, he received the first Atoms for Peace Award. These awards were well deserved by the greatest scientist Denmark had ever produced.

In 1975, Niels Bohr's son, Aage Bohr, was awarded the Nobel Prize in physics with Benjamin Mottlesen, also a Danish citizen. The two scientists are associated with the institute founded by Aage Bohr's illustrious father.

A sum of more than a billion kroner a year in Denmark is allocated to scientific research, which today is assuming a more practical thrust—such as practical applications for nuclear energy, generation of power from other sources than coal and oil, agricultural research for improvement of crops, and studies in critical ecological problems.

One-third of the scientific subsidy goes to universities and other research centers, such as the Meteorological Institute, the Geodetic Institute, the Carlsberg Laboratory, and the Technical University, located at Lyngby, north of Copenhagen.

Another third of the annual science subsidy goes to research being carried out at Risø Atomic Energy Laboratory near Roskilde and to private institutions. At Risø, the nation's most costly science center, eight hundred staff members are engaged in working out methods for applying atomic energy to peaceful uses.

The final third of the annual science subsidies is given to large corporations for their work in the development of new scientific products.

Even this large amount set aside for research is not enough in terms of the gross national product. Denmark plans to increase the research allotment each year—the target being 2.5 percent of GNP by 1985.

One area of scientific research in Denmark is becoming a highly controversial matter—nuclear power. The proposed construction of nuclear power plants has brought forth loud protests from some sectors as well as cries of acclaim from others. The problem seems to be what to do with the nuclear waste in such a small country and how to prevent the serious possibility that the health of the populace will be affected. As in other countries, this issue will take time to be resolved.

Scientific research plays an increasingly important role in Denmark. Not only does it serve to strengthen the economy but also to apply new approaches in the area of social sciences that may eventually help solve some of the modern problems that exist in every part of the globe.

Tools of the furniture craftsman and examples of Danish design

CHAPTER 16

APPLIED ARTS AND HANDICRAFTS

WHERE ARE SOME of the largest summertime crowds in Copenhagen? In Tivoli, yes. In restaurants, yes. But what about the stores? Probably the most popular places, at least for tourists, are those shops and counters specializing in the sale of Danish figurines, plates, furniture, glassware, silver, textiles, stoneware, sweaters, needlework, and pewter. At these places, it's often very hard to get waited on, so popular are the products of Danish design and craftsmanship. Also well-visited today are the factories that turn out these attractive items, and few tour companies do not include at least one or two of these fascinating attractions in their itinerary.

Although Danish craftsmanship dates back as far as the sixteenth century or beyond, Danish applied arts and industrial design have come to real international fame just recently.

An exception might be claimed by the Royal Copenhagen Porcelain Factory, which has had international renown for more than two centuries. Its beginnings go back to the 1760s, when the royal family became interested in the secret of Chinese hardpaste porcelain and procured a French ceramist to work on it, only to have a Danish chemist, twelve years later, discover the secret on his own. Records show that the Copenhagen factory was founded in 1775 and was taken over by the crown four years later.

A costly Flora Danica dinner service of Royal Copenhagen porcelain is on display at Rosenborg Palace. The set was ordered by Frederik VI in 1790, while he was still Crown Prince. It took thirteen years to complete the twenty-six hundred pieces of this magnificent service, which is still used by the royal family on special occasions.

The now-famous Danish blue underglazed porcelain products did not attract international attention until 1889, when they won a *grand prix* at the world exhibition in Paris. The credit then, in large measure, was due to the decorative work of artist Arnold Krog (1856-1931), who introduced a special painting technique to beautify the items.

With those two exceptions, applied art in Denmark is largely a twentieth-century development. Applied art is born from a desire to satisfy a need. Whether that need is utilitarian or aesthetic is immaterial, although the artistic interests of the designer—and probably the public—are better served if the need is both aesthetic and utilitarian. That is, the finished product should express both beauty and usefulness. In fact, in order for the field of applied arts to be a successful venture, all the various aspects of the production should be well balanced—the quality of the raw materials, the aesthetic design, the craftsmanship, the economy, and, in many cases, the packaging. The Danes, with their love of discovery, their appreciation of simple beauty and genuineness, as well as their frugality, seem to have found a real forte in the area of industrial design.

For raw material, Denmark has traditionally utilized the old "naturals"—wood, cotton, wool, silver, tin, glass, clay, copper, and stone—with excellent results. Now the Danes are adding to those substances the new manufactured products—plastics, cardboard, acrylic, foam rubber, melamine, urethane, and others (sometimes to the distress of conservative artists)—and developing avant-garde ideas in uses and combinations of materials.

From the wide subject of Danish applied arts—on which at least a volume could be written—only four areas of achievement will be considered in this chapter—porcelain, silver, glass, and furniture. Plan to explore the rest in person —the prints, textiles, book designs, sweaters, stoneware, stainless steel, pewter, all things of Danish design.

First, there's the Royal Copenhagen porcelain, which, as already mentioned, was the international attention-getter at the Paris world exhibition of 1889. In the year 1900, the rival Danish porcelain company, Bing and Grøndahl (organized in 1853) had a similar *grand prix* triumph with ceramics by J. F. Willumsen (1863-1958). The Bing and Grøndahl trademark is a tiny three-towered castle; the Royal Copenhagen trademark is three small, wavy lines, signifying Denmark's three waterways—the Great Belt, the Little Belt, and the Sound.

Part of the secret of the beautiful porcelain from both these companies lies in the raw materials used, but certainly a great deal of the credit goes to the special underglaze technique and to the artists who design and apply the decorative patterns.

Originally, the work was limited to dinner services and such—first in a spidery, Oriental motif, then in diverse patterns of floral and gull designs. Later the work was expanded to include vases and painted figurines—exquisite statuettes, all painstakingly handpainted, all underglazed in soft-colored pigments, especially blues, browns, and grays. In spite of their high prices, these pieces of Danish porcelain are still much in demand.

Since the Danes have always had a special love of Christmas, celebrating it so gaily and so long each year, it is natural they should conceive the notion of the annual Christmas plate, an idea that has become very popular today. It was in 1895 that the Bing and Grøndahl factory first decided to make a Christmas plate, opening the design competition to its employees. Ever since that year, a new pattern for the seven-inch plate has been selected annually. The mold is destroyed after production.

In the year 1908, the Royal Copenhagen Factory followed suit—using, of course, a different pattern, as well as a bordered edge. The plates of the two companies are equally in demand today—partly by reason of their beautiful Danish motifs and partly because of their scarcity and ever-increasing value, which make them good collector's items. Artists compete annually for the design selected by the two companies for their Christmas plates. Subjects vary greatly—from picturesque landscapes to favorite churches and meaningful Christmas scenes, all with a distinctly Danish flavor. Special commemorative plates have been added, including the *Mors Dag* (Mother's Day) plate and the Olympiad plate, issued on the occasion of the 1972 Olympic Games in Munich. In 1975 a series of "bicentennial" plates was begun. The first one celebrated the founding of the Royal Copenhagen factory. The 1976 plate commemorates the bicentennial of the independence of the United States.

Contemporary materials and interesting modern designs began making their successful appearance in Danish porcelain in the 1930s with the emergence of the design philosophy called functionalism. In ceramics, this trend leads away from a pictorial style and toward a textural style, dependent in part on the richness of the varicolored glazes. Leading contemporary ceramists include Natalie Krebs, famous for glazes; Axel Salto, for integration of materials, forms, and decoration; Gertrud Vasegaard, for perpetuation of traditional styles through stoneware; Christian Paulsen, for simplification of design in stoneware; and Erik Magnussen, for extreme simplicity in porcelain. While this new trend has certainly not replaced the traditional mode in Danish ceramics, it has added immeasurably to the dimensions of Danish applied arts.

The distinctiveness of Danish silver sprang initially from the work of one great sculptor and silversmith, Georg Jensen (1866-1935). Jensen's abilities as a craftsman and an artist helped applied artists gain wider acceptance and profit for their work, not only in Denmark but in other countries as well. Artistically, Jensen created a new, individual style in silverware—partially a reflection of the international style known as Art Nouveau (1893-1910), which strove for originality and utilized chiefly flowing, curvilinear patterns.

Modern Danish silverware, like ceramics, has responded to the trend of functionalism. The chief artistic criterion may still be: is the item attractive? But close corollaries now are: is it simple? and is it easy to use? Sculptor Henning Koppel's name is seen among those of the important silver artists today, especially because of his beautiful and useful hollowware. So are the names of Søren Georg Jensen and Kay Bøjesen. All three of these artists worked as students under Georg Jensen. It was Bøjesen who stressed the importance of making utilitarian items out of silver because the metal grows more lustrous with daily use.

Many shoppers—and window-shoppers—dearly love the silver of Georg Jensen, Hans Hansen, A. Michelsen, and those just mentioned, but they may not love the dear prices! They are top level—at least on Strøget (The Copenhagen Mall). However, one might also observe that the simplicity of Danish silver is reminiscent of Early American design. Thus the bride of today may well use her mother's or her grandmother's silverware with new Danish modern because of the neat transition of the Danish pattern from the traditional to the contemporary.

This might be a good time to consider the famous Danish Christmas spoons. These lovely creations were developed by artists in the A. Michelsen Company in Copenhagen. The company first issued a commemorative sterling silver dessert spoon in 1898 in honor of King Christian's eightieth birthday. The idea was so well received that the company continued to make souvenir spoons for various occasions. Soon, in light of their popularity, someone suggested making Christmas spoons, with a new design for each year, a plan similar to the one for ceramic plates. And from 1910 to this day, not a year's issue has been missed.

If you are interested in completing a table setting in modern Danish style, you will have no trouble in locating a coordinating pattern in glassware; for, while there is now in Denmark considerable emphasis on the production and export of plain, strong glass suitable for industrial and architectural purposes, there is also increasing focus on designing and manufacturing attractive table glassware.

Some glass factories, like the famous Holmegaard in Fensmark, in Zealand, advertise that their glasses are "individually made and blown in a centuries-old tradition." At Holmegaard, table glasses are made in a variety of lovely shapes, all designed for the glass factory by well-known artists. The newly designed Danish Skibsglas of simple, sturdy design is extremely popular. Other patterns include Almue, Mandalay, Balloon, Tivoli, Mazurka, Stub, and Flutes.

Best known among Denmark's industrial arts, and most generally identified with the term Danish Modern, is Danish furniture. During the late nineteenth and early twentieth century, furniture styles became a mixture of periods and designs, and furniture was generally impractical. To change this unfortunate trend, a group of leading furniture craftsmen, who called themselves the Copenhagen Cabinetmakers Guild, collaborated with outstanding artists to promote more distinctive and more functional furniture.

One of the leaders of the movement was architect Kaare Klint, who founded a school for talented young designers at the Royal Danish Academy of Fine Arts. Klint pointed the way toward the development of a clean-lined style, a rational approach, and a careful concern for usefulness. Other famous designers who joined him in spearheading this "renaissance" in furniture modes were Hans J. Wegner, Børge Mogensen, Finn Juhl, Steen Rasmussen, and Ole Wanscher—all of whose names have become distinguished trademarks in Danish furniture design.

For years, the organization of craftsmen and designers exhibited their work annually at Guild exhibitions, through which the styles in furniture acquired recognition throughout Denmark and abroad. The Danish furniture industry responded to public enthusiasm for its new patterns, with the result that by the mid-1950s the great demand put eight hundred factories into operation, working full speed to fill orders. Denmark became then, as it is today, one of the leading countries in designing and exporting furniture.

Danish Modern brought other recognized artists to the field of furniture design. Arne Jacobsen. a well-known international architect, extended his talents in numerous directions, including that of furniture designing. (See also chapter 11.) A notable example of his pioneering contribution in this field is his invention of the "egg" and the "ant" design in chairs.

New ideas and new designers are constantly gaining prominence in Danish furniture making, but the finished products always have quality workmanship and aesthetic refinement. Experimenting with more manufactured materials is Poul Cadovius, who owns two large furniture manufacturing firms himself. Two of the most modern designers are Ninna Ditzel, whose latest interest is in the use of plastics for furniture— an experiment which builds a kind of geometric, synthetic landscape in a room—and designer Jørgen Høj, who builds a fantastic party group of furniture with aluminum rings and cushions.

Danish ingenuity suggests the name of one more designer, Piet Hein, mentioned earlier as a clever poet. Hein is also a famous mathematician and engineer. At one end of the long list of his inventions is the small super-egg, a drink cooler, made in brass or silver and purchased by thousands for a gift or conversation piece. At the other end of the list is his large super-ellipsoid plan for buildings and larger structures, such as the new city center in Stockholm, Sweden. Finding that this super-ellipse shape, which falls between that of the ellipse and the rectangle, can be used to advantage for many curved objects, Piet Hein continues to devote his scientific knowledge in the construction of super-elliptical furniture, dishes, coasters, lamps, silverware, textile patterns, and even simple toys.

One excellent outlet for Danish arts is the organization known as Den Permanente, which is run by some 280 Danish craftsmen, designers, and firms engaged in the production of industrial art. It maintains a permanent sales exhibition on Vesterbrogade in Copenhagen. All the products displayed in this beautiful store have been approved and accepted by an impartial committee of the association called the "Permanent Exhibition of Danish Arts and Crafts and Industrial Design," established in 1931. Den Permanente is a private foundation, owned by its members, most of whom have their own workshops. The organization is unique in that the profits must be used for the improvement and expansion of the organization's activities. Departments in the store include those of furniture, textiles, ceramics, jewelry, lamps, glass, paintings, and sculpture. At present, some forty-six thousand individual designs are included. Also, the store's wholesale export department deals with retailers in more than fifty countries.

Denmark, Norway, and Sweden have united in forming the PLUS Centre, a nonprofit organization that works for cooperation among designers, craftsmen, and the industry as a whole, with the aim of raising the standards of their products. The PLUS Centre is housed in the old fortress of Frederikstad, located between Oslo and the Swedish border, in the castle originally built by Denmark's King Frederik II as a protection against the Swedes. Now the stately structure has become one of the most important citadels for Scandinavian cooperation—the development of good design and craftsmanship.

Since 1949, the Scandinavians have presented their best items every year at the Scandinavian Furniture Fair in Copenhagen. It is here that furniture buyers come to see what people will be sitting on or eating at for years to come.

So, even in the world market of the industrial arts, Denmark has gained an enviable role, which is watched internationally with respect and admiration.

The great storyteller Hans Christian Andersen
Inserts: Novelist Isak Dinesen
Philosopher Søren Kierkegaard

CHAPTER 17

THE SPOKEN AND WRITTEN WORD

VICTOR BORGE, Danish humorist and musician, is fond of saying, "Danish is not a language. It is a disease of the throat."

True, Danish is quite a guttural language. It involves the use of the uvular *r* and a number of "back vowels." Try practicing an order for the delicious Danish dessert, *Rødgrød med Fløde på,* and your throat may actually get sore! But difficulty with the new sounds is a very temporary matter and should not deter you from learning the language if you wish. It is really not too hard to master, especially if you have some knowledge of German.

Though there is a close similarity in vocabulary among all the Scandinavian languages, the Danish language has several distinguishing features in addition to its guttural *r* and its lack of melody. There is a weakening of the sounds *p, t,* and *k* to *b, d,* and *g,* and also a peculiar use of the glottal stop. Also, there are three vowels in the language that are not found in English: *ae* (pronounced as a drawn-out ɛ); *ø* (pronounced *er* without the *r*); and *å,* formerly *aa* (pronounced as *o* in *or*).

Of all the Scandinavian languages, Danish is the most prone to innovation, and it has changed more than any of the others throughout the years. In fact, it is still changing, particularly by the use of ellipsis and by the adoption of foreign words. For example, the courteous expression, *vaer så god,* used when handing a person something, has now been contracted to *vaersgo.* And you'll find any number of American words—like *weekend, start,* and *undermine*—in daily use.

In years past, a different dialect was to be found in Jutland and on every inhabited island, particularly in rural communities. Zealanders could hardly understand Jutlanders and vice versa; visitors from other lands were utterly confused. But today the various dialects are fading out. With the drop in rural population, the use of fast transportation, and the advent of radio and television, Danish dialects are hardly noticeable.

The Danish language has been in use a long time. Runic inscriptions date back to the fourth century, and Icelandic poetry to the tenth century. Words and spellings from other areas—notably Scotland, Germany, and Holland—are in evidence in these early writings, but the basic language is clearly Danish.

Now, what have the Danes accomplished with their language? In other words, if one were asked, "What is the most important field of Danish literary contribution in the nearly thousand years of recorded writing," what would the answer be? It might well be, "The area of poetic expression."

At first, this reply may seem too limited. It would exclude the valuable scientific treatises, the historical documents, the news accounts, and the numerous philosophical writings of which there have been so many masterpieces.

But even so, the area of poetic expression covers quite an expanse. It includes ballads and folk songs, hymns, powerful and witty dramas, poetry, stories, novels, and fairy tales—all of which have done so much to give Denmark its share of literary distinction and are so typical of its sensitive, imaginative people.

Take the ballads, for example. No country has a finer collection. There are more than five hundred and fifty of them in existence—three thousand, in fact, if one includes the numerous variations. Like the English and Scottish ballads, their authorship is unknown, but quite a number are thought to have been chanted and sung in Viking days and to have come down by word of mouth.

The Norse ballads have a lilting rhythm and meter and stanzas of two to four lines. Even a ballad with a tragic plot may carry a jingling refrain. The stories may relate to gods and goddesses, heroes and kings, knights and ladies, violence and romance, or magic and witchcraft.

Ballads are meant to be sung and preferably danced to, with the leader sometimes singing the verses and the rest of the party coming in on the chorus:

I saw a sail fare o'er the Sound
(So many a pennon of gold)
There sailed the Knight Strange with Dagmar the Queen.

The Knight and Sir Strange they sat at the board,
(So many a pennon of gold)
There spake they so many a jesting word.
There sailed the Knight Strange with Dagmar the Queen.

Lithe now and listen, Sir Strange, to me,
(So many a pennon of gold)
Thou shalt fare to Bejerland and woo a maid for me.
There sailed Sir Strange with Dagmar the Queen.

Folk songs and ballads have always been so popular that at times even the clergy have taken to them with enthusiasm. The story is told about one famous member of the cloth, Anders Arrebo (born in 1587), who lived to regret his love of lively expression. When he was only twenty-three years old, he became pastor at the royal court; at thirty, he became Bishop of Tronhjem. His style of speaking was youthful. His whole manner was youthful. Once, at a wedding party, he threw off his pastoral robes and began to sing folk songs and dance an accompaniment. But this exhibition was too much for Arrebo's enemies, who were probably envious of his youthful eminence and wanted to see him deposed. They exerted enough pressure on the king to have him removed from his position.

Incidentally, in his retreat at Malmø, Arrebo may not have danced, but he did produce some lasting literary gems. He translated a number of Psalms and set them to familiar tunes, and he wrote a long epic poem, *Hexaemeron,* depicting the creation of the world in six days.

In view of the fact that church attendance in Denmark today is at low ebb, it is interesting that the Danes have a vast heritage of hymns to their literary credit. Of course, church-going used to be the thing to do—in fact, for some time it was compulsory, and the Danes love to sing whenever they assemble.

Back in the seventeenth century, Bishop Thomas Kingo stood out as a leading writer and collector of hymns. The collection that he dedicated to the queen probably helped to make him Bishop of Funen. Another bishop, Hans Brorson, Bishop of Ribe, serving the oldest cathedral of Denmark, also wrote hymns that are among Denmark's best known. Because his congregation had been using only German hymns, Brorson felt the need for a hymnal in the Danish language and set about writing and compiling *Troens Rare Klenodie* (Beautiful Music of Faith). So outstanding was this contribution to poetic literature that, aside from satirical verse, it is considered the best of Denmark's eighteenth-century poetry. If you were to attend a Danish church today, it is more than likely you would sing one of Hans Brorson's hymns.

Although there were many writers of hymns and religious poetry during the religious revival of the nineteenth century, the names of Christian Richardt, Steen Steensen Blicher, N. F. S. Grundtvig, Christian Winther, and B. S. Ingemann stand out as exemplary.

The field of drama has also been important to the people of Denmark. This kind of literature—in Latin, to be sure—began to appear in Denmark during the sixteenth century as miracle, mystery, and morality plays. Many of these plays have been lost, but the fact that some of them remain testifies to an early interest among the Danes for a poetic portrayal of ideas and feelings.

The real dawn of Danish dramatic literature came in the early eighteenth century. It began in the work of Ludvig Holberg (1684-1754). Holberg was Norwegian by birth. When he was still in his teens, he left his home in Bergen to try his luck in other lands—Denmark, Holland, England, France, and Italy. After studying and wandering about for years, he returned to Denmark, where at age thirty-two he obtained a university position in the department of metaphysics, and, later, in his favorite subject, history.

This man was destined to be one of the most influential literary figures to come out of Scandinavia. Norway, as well as Denmark, claims him as its native son. When you visit Bergen, the residents will point out to you an impressive statue of Holberg, which dominates one of the city squares.

Oddly enough, before his thirty-fifth year, this versatile man, who was to produce so many kinds of literature, had had no interest at all in poetry. In fact, it bored him. Then, in 1719, after very little study and less practice in that area, he was somehow motivated to write *Peder Paars,* a long, humorous, narrative poem. Suddenly, he found himself acclaimed as a full-fledged writer of comedy.

The elaborate, satirical poem begins as a parody on classical epic poetry, specifically Vergil's *Aeneid.* As the story progresses, corruption, social weaknesses, pedantry, and hypocrisy are all subjected to good-humored ridicule. Though the piece was widely enjoyed and applauded when presented on stage, it was also denounced by many as a shocking attack on good people and on the entire field of literary academia. These critics sought to suppress it, but King Frederik IV was amused by it and endorsed its publication.

Before this time there had been no Danish theater as such, only court performances of Italian and French pieces for royalty and the nobility. For commoners, there were only lightweight pantomimes, wandering shows and such things as "strong-man acts"—no real dramatic productions worthy of the name. Now, with the encouragement of Ludvig Holberg, a true Danish theater was opened in Copenhagen on September 23, 1722.

For the first performance, the play chosen was Holberg's *Den Politiske Kandestøber* (The Political Tinman). As soon as the play was announced, there was great public excitement, and on opening night the theater was packed to capacity; in fact, many had to be turned away. Those who were lucky enough to get in were wild with enthusiasm. The author was nearly wild with delight! He went home and immediately set about writing the next play. From 1722 to 1725, Holberg supplied that theater—free of charge—with some twenty plays from his own pen, most of them satires and all of them comedies.

By his own admission, Holberg sought to ridicule human

and institutional foibles and help eradicate them. Undoubtedly, his most famous, most effective play was *Jeppe paa
Bjerget* (Jeppe on the Mountain), which has been translated into many languages. It portrays a poor drunken
peasant who has been suddenly transported from his miser-
able life to one of luxury, fame, and honor. In his new
surroundings, he is the epitome of wretchedness, a pitiable
figure who does not know where to turn or how to act.
While the play has many laughs at the expense of the peasant, it was not intended to ridicule peasants themselves, but
rather the glamorized treatment of them that the romantic
movement in literature was subjecting them to.

Another Danish dramatist, renowned throughout Scandinavia and abroad, was Adam Oehlenschlaeger—a brilliant
leader in Denmark's era of romanticism early in the nineteenth century.

Of all his plays, his most famous undoubtedly is *Håkon
Jarl,* modeled after Greek tragedies and rich in expressions
of humanism. Other plays of Oehlenschlaeger's that have
enjoyed wide popularity, many of them in foreign countries,
are *Canute the Great, The Varangians in Constantinople,
Tordenskjold,* and *Socrates. Socrates* was probably the playwright's favorite. And Hans Christian Andersen mentioned
this play in his account of Oehlenschlaeger's death:

> His death was without pain; his children stood around
> him and he asked them to read aloud from his tragedy,
> *Socrates,* where he speaks of immortality and assurance
> of eternal life. He was quiet, and prayed that the agony
> might not be hard, laid down his head and died.

For most of the nineteenth century, Denmark ranked with
England and Germany in outstanding theater. Consider
Heiberg, another of the country's greats. Johan Heiberg

was a dramatist and an undisputed drama critic, flourishing from 1826 to 1860, and his wife, Johanne Luise, was one of the most accomplished actresses of the century. They made quite a team.

Heiberg usually selected material that could be treated with a light touch, and he wrote sparkling dialogue for it, often setting it to music. His fairy tale plays were delightful —especially *Seven Sleepers' Day* and *Elf Hill*—which may still be seen from time to time.

It is unfortunate, but perhaps natural, that Heiberg and the "fairy tale man," Hans Christian Andersen, did not get along too well together, even though they both enjoyed the same poetic medium—the drama. One time, Andersen wrote a beautiful dramatic story, entitled *Fortune's Flower,* and submitted it to the theater in which Heiberg was censor. Heiberg rejected it with stinging comment. To retaliate, Andersen wrote another play, *The Lying-In Room,* and sent it anonymously to Heiberg, who immediately accepted it and cast his wife, Luise, in the title role. The play with the unknown author ran for more than a year with great success, much to the secret delight of Hans Christian Andersen.

One day he approached the director of the theater to find out if his previously submitted play, *Fortune's Flower,* was being reconsidered. The director replied, "No, we definitely can't use it. Now if you could write a piece like *The Lying-In Room,* well—!" Even then Andersen did not tell the secret, and it was years before he did.

Heiberg lived to regret his failure to endorse his colleague's writings, for Andersen's fame far surpassed that of his critics and most of his contemporaries.

However, Andersen's pinnacle of success was not reached in drama but in the realm of fairy tale. His vast collection of fantastic tales, exciting in plot and often fanciful in setting, immediately delighted the children he loved to gather around himself. The stories were soon written down, and today the best of them are to be found in the language of every civilized country in the world.

Andersen really wrote for grown-ups as well as children. He stated his objective in these words: "I grab an idea to appeal to adults, then tell the story to the youngsters while I remember that Father and Mother often listen in, and they must be given food for thought."

Sometimes Andersen told his stories from the stage, reading to capacity crowds. He would begin his program with such words as these, spelling out the task of the poet:

> Through all men's lives there runs an invisible thread that shows we belong to God. To find this thread, the poet's art must help us. It comes in many shapes. Holberg let it come in his comedies, showing us the men in his time—their weaknesses and their amusing qualities. In the earliest times, the poet's art dealt mostly with what we call wonder stories. The Bible itself has enclosed wisdom and truth in parables and allegories, not to be taken literally but according to their significance—the invisible thread running through them. When one calls out to the rocks and cliffs and hears an echo, it is not really the rocks that respond, but our own voices. So with wonder stories. They resound in our hearts what we have felt all along and echo the true meaning for our enrichment.

Twentieth-century Danish drama has shown a radical departure from the romanticism of the nineteenth century. Playwrights range from Kai Munk, the martyred pastor-author who wrote the masterful ten-act drama *Herod,* to such men as the controversial C. E. Soya, who was influenced by Freud, and Kjeld Abell, whose plays run the gamut from satire to powerful personal message. They also include a whole generation of so-called "angry young men," exemplified by the versatile and provocative Klaus Rifbjerg. All have had a marked impact on the Danish theater and Danish thought.

Many of the Danish playwrights wrote poems, too—Oehlenschlaeger, Andersen, Heiberg, Hertz, Munk, and Rifbjerg, for example—and it's sometimes hard to say in which medium they excelled.

Oehlenschlaeger is said to have ushered in the Danish Golden Age of Romanticism in the nineteenth century with his brilliant poem "The Golden Horns." He wrote the poem about the two golden horns that had been unearthed in Slesvig in the seventeenth and eighteenth centuries. The horns bore inscriptions about myths dating back to Viking days. Oehlenschlaeger is the author of the beloved national anthem "There Is a Lovely Land."

Kai Munk's literary talents lay equally in prose and poetry. One of his most thrilling poems to the Danes was entitled "To the King." It is his tribute to Christian X, who was so strong a support to Danish morale during the German occupation:

> Once more today you ride your city round,
> Graciously, like a king and like a Dane.
> It does us good, it seems to say to us
> That Denmark still is sitting in the saddle.
> Our rallying point you've always been as now
> The decades through, in hardship as in weal.
> Cabinets have come and gone and come again,
> The king stayed on unchanged, and in this chill
> Bright April morning he is with us now.

Your smile is gone, but still your glancing eye
Surveys the kingdom—though no longer free,
It still is yours, its fortune too is yours.

When Denmark's tongue speaks out with most effect,
It stirs us in the echo of our hymns,
And from our hymns we learn that he who waits
In silence may be doing all he should.
That bishop's word is now a royal word:
To wait in silence with a faithful heart
For what, as we all know, we long for most
In faith that he who longs for what is right
Will see the due fulfillment of his wish.
Good day, King Christian, and good day-to-be!

About a century ago a colony of German literary men led
by Friedrich Klopstock lived in Copenhagen. They were
important to Danish literature chiefly because of their impact on Johnnes Ewald, one of the most significant literary
figures Denmark has produced. Ewald's whole life reads
like a story—from his early Robinson Crusoe experiences
and unrequited love to his Horatio Alger triumphs in the
world of letters and dramas. His 1870 musical, *Fiskerne*
(The Fishermen), sealed his success. One of the most tuneful
of its lyrics became one of the national anthems—*"Kong
Christian Stod ved Højen Mast."* (See chapter 3.)

Outstanding Danish poets of the present century are more
scarce, but among the best-known names are Nils Petersen
(Kai Munk's cousin), an idealistic lyric poet; Thorvald
Bjørnvig, famous for philosophical symbolism; versatile
Klaus Rifbjerg; and Piet Hein, who has completely cap-
tured the hearts of his readers with his gem-like grooks.

Of course, Danish literary expression has not been limited
to poems. Prose writers too have made a contribution to

literature. Steen Steensen Blicher (1782-1848), who is considered by many to be the forerunner of modern realistic prose, was one of the first to discover that the Jutland heath had rich literary material and that its inhabitants were warm, lovable people of which great stories should be made. He wrote about the west coast fisherfolk in *Marie,* of proprietors in *Høstferierne,* of peasants in *Hosekraemmerne,* of clergymen in *Praesten i Vejlby.* Unfortunately, Blicher did not gain recognition until after his death. Now, in his memory, the manor of Herningsholm in Jutland is being restored as a museum to contain the originals of his many works.

Georg Brandes, who succeeded Johan Heiberg as official literary critic in 1871, was a staunch champion of the importance of good literary substance in contrast to form and a devotee of realistic idealism. Although Brandes made numerous enemies, many young Danish writers owed their success to his guidance. Because his works have themes on social problems, much social reform came about as the result of his literary leadership.

From this point on, Denmark's literature began to reflect two main areas of concern—current world problems and the Danes' feeling for their heritage. These themes have carried over into the twentieth century as well.

Sophus Schandorff, a realistic novelist and a disciple of Brandes, depicted with sympathetic understanding the life of the Zealandic peasant and satirized academia and the government. Copenhagener Karl Larsen was a master of psychological fiction. He proved himself expert at depicting character types and unsavory milieus. Herman Bang was a successful writer of short sketches—impressionistic and often tragic—all showing his keen sensitivity to human sorrow and misery.

Joint winners of the 1917 Nobel Prize for literature were

Henrik Pontoppidan and Karl Gjellerup. Pontoppidan was essentially a pessimist, devoted to the idea that the responsibility of the literary world is to present a photographic view of life as it is lived. Gjellerup was a powerful writer of dramas and novels who attacked Georg Brandes' ideas.

Certain traits stand out as especially characteristic of modern writing in Denmark: first, it marks a definite break with literary tradition; and second, it is a revolt of writers from the provinces against Copenhagen's literary domination.

Among the writers from the provinces, four Jutlanders are exemplary for their contributions: Johannes V. Jensen, Johan Skjoldborg, Harry Soiberg, and Jeppe Aakjaer. Of especially strong influence on modern Danish writers was Johannes Jensen, who was awarded the Nobel Prize for literature in 1944.

Another writer reflecting an innovative literary trend was Martin Andersen Nexø from the island of Bornholm. Himself of poor family, Nexø championed the cause of social reform. He wrote stories of city laborers, fishermen, hoboes—men and women who manage to preserve their human worth under adverse conditions.

It is natural that the worldwide turmoil of the twentieth century should show up in Danish literary expression, as it has all over the world. Jacob Paludan, for instance, was moved to write stories reflecting a quest for values and for faith in civilized guidelines to an ordered society. His books *Jørgen Stein, Birds of the Lighthouse,* and *Ripening Fields* are considered masterpieces.

From quite another point of view, Tom Kristensen's novel *Havoc,* written in a contemporary style, is a bitter denunciation of Danish neutrality during the world wars. His poem "Atlantis" develops the idea that a new and improved social order will come only after a complete breakdown of the old order.

Marxist Hans Kirk wrote a controversial book, *The Fisherman,* that led to his internment for Communistic leanings. But Kirk continued to write, following up *The Fisherman* with *The Slave,* dealing with dictatorship, and *The Son of Wrath,* dealing with Jesus Christ as a revolutionary. His books continue to be popular.

The German occupation during World War II, which caused so much anxiety and insecurity, gave rise to much Danish writing. For example, there was H. C. Branner, novelist and playwright, who dealt expertly with human reactions in *No One Knows the Night,* and William Heinesen, who handled a similar theme in the story of *The Black Saucepan.* Heinesen has written more than forty novels, some of which have been translated into English.

Karen Blixen (using the pseudonym Isak Dinesen), who died in 1974 at age eighty-nine, was quite unusual in that she wrote first in English, not in her native tongue, and then translated her work into Danish. Her autobiographical book, *Out of Africa,* is a realistic account of current situations in Kenya, but it is based on Blixen's belief that life on earth is a drama devised by God.

The person labeled "the most Danish" of all modern men and women of letters is Martin Hansen. If his fame were to rest on only one work, the novel *The Liar,* alone, which deals with appreciation of old culture, would be sufficient to place his name among literary stars. Hansen was the first to receive the Laurels Award now given yearly by the large Danish booksellers' club, *Boghandlerklubben.*

One of the most controversial books published in the early 1970s was Henrik Stangerup's incisive novel, *Manden Der Vilde Vaere Skyldig* (The Man Who Would Be Responsible), which came out on the heels of his *Løgn over Løgn* (Lie upon Lie). *Manden* is sharply satirical of a society that relieves people of their own individual decisions and makes them products of a system.

As this chapter has hinted, the Danes are devoted to books. They are definitely a reading people. Excellent libraries abound—both research libraries at the universities and local libraries for the general public. Two impressive facts stand out concerning Denmark's language and literature: Denmark publishes more books per capita per year than any other nation, and there are virtually *no* illiterate Danes.

The Thorvaldsen Museum in Copenhagen
Insert: Bertel Thorvaldsen

CHAPTER 18

AN ARTISTIC NATION

WHILE ALL DANES do not profess to be connoisseurs of art, they do, on the whole, take art seriously. Visitors to Denmark are always surprised to find so many and such varied museums, not only in Copenhagen but in all parts of the country. The nearly two hundred museums in Denmark demonstrate the interest and support of the Danish people for the cultural life. When Denmark was host to the International Congress of Museums in June of 1974, no less than 165 museums were showing outstanding exhibits for the benefit of conference members and visitors. Comprehensive displays of all the cultural arts, from antiquity to the present day, from artifacts to masterpieces of art by Danish and internationally known artists, were included in the temporary and permanent collections during this open exhibition.

During the last fifteen years, cultural policy has undergone some radical changes that have affected both the activities and the attitudes of the Danish people. The establishment of a Ministry of Cultural Affairs in 1961 was the first major step in an attempt to meet the cultural needs of a contemporary society. The second effort was the passage in 1964 of the National Art Fund Act, establishing support of art, literature, and music through monetary grants to young writers and artists and to museums for the purchase of paintings and other art forms.

The purpose of the state funds is primarily to help provide opportunities in all the fields of art and to stimulate local communities to expand or build facilities to house significant art works and to afford meeting places for classes, seminars, and concerts.

The recently remodeled National Museum of Fine Arts, located in a beautiful park in Copenhagen, is Denmark's oldest and largest art museum. Collections include works of Rembrandt, Rubens, Matisse, and many other foreign notables, in addition to works by prominent Danish artists. Here you may trace the development of Danish painting from the Middle Ages to the present time—an excellent presentation of foreign and national influences on the art of the day.

Another popular art museum in Copenhagen is the stately Ny Carlsberg Glyptotek, founded in 1888 by Carl Jacobsen, owner of the Carlsberg Breweries. This museum contains a large collection of paintings and sculptures of international note, as well as representative works of most of the nineteenth-century Danish painters.

Not until the early part of the eighteenth century was there any native Danish art produced. With the establishment of the Royal Academy of Fine Arts in 1754, Danish art began to emerge under the leadership of two notable painters—N. A. Abildgaard (1743-1809), a neoclassicist, and Jens Juel (1745-1802), a revolutionist in art. Juel was also distinguished for founding the National School of Portrait Painting.

C. W. Eckersberg (1783-1853), sometimes called the "father of Danish painting," pioneered a trend that influenced painters for many generations. At J. S. David's school in Paris, where Eckersberg studied, he was taught to observe nature deeply and penetratingly. As professor at the

Academy of Fine Arts in Copenhagen, he taught his students the same thing—the art of keen vision. Eckersberg was a prolific painter, and all of his paintings, including many of the sea and sailing ships, demonstrate his unmatched attention to detail. In his use of cool, light colors in lovely seasonal landscapes and seascapes, Eckersberg reflects the true Danish spirit.

After the 1878 World Exhibition of Art in Paris, the age of realism took hold in Denmark, and artists turned to the open air, where they began to paint modern life in the out-of-doors.

The Skagen Museum, located on the North Sea coast of Jutland, exhibits works of the Skagen painters, who founded a new school of expression in the late nineteenth century. Skagen, the remote yet picturesque point at the tip of Jutland, where the Kattegat and Skagerrak meet in the challenge of the sea, had become a painter's paradise.

P. S. Krøyer, a master painter even at age twenty, spearheaded the movement in paintings of toilers, peasants, and fishermen of Skagen. Occasionally impressionistic, he reflected the moods of the people and the sea.

Michael Ancher, another Skagen artist, who similarly painted the sea and fishermen, developed his manly characters effectively in dramatic settings. While staying in the Skagen area, Ancher met the innkeeper's daughter and gave her painting lessons. Later, as Anna Ancher, she too became an artist, portraying in a sensitive and warm way the inner life of the people as they worked within home or shop. In recent years her works have attracted so much attention that the Skagen Museum has devoted a separate room to a collection of her paintings.

Vilhelm Hammershøj (1864-1916), was the leading figure of the symbolism movement. The artists in this movement expressed their individual feelings on spiritual themes symbolically, through the use of expressive lines and large, unbroken composition. Hammershøj's stylized geometric form became well known, as did the subjects he used—a number of interiors of old houses in Copenhagen.

The paintings of J. F. Willumsen (1863-1958) helped introduce a new element in Danish art. His compositions portray the theme of the strength of nature and the weakness of human beings, but they carry the assurance that we will eventually conquer nature. Though he lived most of his life in France, Willumsen was nevertheless the central figure in Danish art for nearly seventy years. Most of his paintings and sculptures are now exhibited in a museum erected for him in Frederikssund just after World War II.

Many of the works of Christian Dalsgaard (1824-1907) are exhibited in the museum of Sorø Academy. Dalsgaard's paintings introduced the theme of folk life, including the *hyggelig* element, into his favorite compositions of interiors. He brings out effectively a warm, human element in his touching but realistic portrayal of the home.

In the Skovgaard Museum, not far from Viborg Cathedral, several generations of the Skovgaard artist family are represented by numerous works. The elder Skovgaard, P. C. Skovgaard (1817-1875), was best known for his landscapes and forest scenes. His inspirational portrait of Grundtvig is regarded as one of the artist's masterpieces.

Skovgaard's sons, Joachim and Niels, also were painters. Their art shows the deep-rooted, traditional influence of their father, yet something of the spirit of their idol, the theologian N. F. S. Grundtvig. Joachim distinguished himself in several powerful works of ecclesiastical art, some of the greatest being the frescoes in the Viborg Cathedral. Here he portrayed scenes from the Old and New Testaments. His almost childlike interpretations of the Bible stories in this large work (he painted five hundred figures on an area of sixteen thousand square feet) bear lasting testimonial to the artist's faith and ardor.

Niels Skovgaard was more meditative in nature but no less imaginative. His excellent altarpiece in the Emanuel Church in Copenhagen, entitled *The Baptism Whitsunday Morning,* is particularly noteworthy.

Joachim Skovgaard's pupil, Niels Larsen Stevns, who worked with him on the cathedral murals, is best known for his portrayal of the life of Hans Christian Andersen in the monumental frescoes in the Andersen Museum at Odense.

The Funen painters were a group of impressionistic artists who painted the idyllic countryside on the island of Funen. Among this group are Johannes Larsen, who portrayed animals and birds and the effects of weather on land and sea, and Poul Christiansen, who is known for his broad, majestic landscapes painted in large bold style and line. The works of these painters and other Funen artists are exhibited in the Funen Stiftsmuseum in Odense, one of the oldest of Danish museums, built in 1885.

Funen artists are also exhibited in the Fåborg Museum, which was founded by Mads Rasmussen in 1910. The Fåborg art building is one of the most distinctive museums in Denmark. A huge statue of Rasmussen stands in the domed hall —a major work of Kai Nielsen (1882-1924), who was himself an outstanding sculptor, born near Odense on Funen.

Asger Jorn (1914-1972) is doubtless the most renowned of contemporary Danish artists, widely acclaimed internationally and represented in museums all over the world. Jorn's work evolved through many experimental phases in all media, as he applied his ceaseless energy to complete a thousand paintings and hundreds of graphics, drawings, tapestries, and sculptures. One of his largest and most famous paintings is *Churchill's Entry into Copenhagen*. Jorn bequeathed most of his own works and his enormous collection—a total of fifty-six hundred pieces—to the Silkeborg Art Museum, located in Jorn's home town in Jutland.

The average visitor to Denmark may overlook one of the most interesting museums in the country—the ultra-modern church and culture center at Nørreland in Holstebro. The Jens Nielsen Art Museum and studio, an integral part of the cube-shaped church complex, were built expressly for the painter, who is still an inspired and active artist in his eighties.

An individualist, whose simple and humorous interpretations of life have labeled him as an impressionist, Nielsen was a late starter in his self-taught painting skill. Most of his paintings have a religious theme—his own unorthodox representations of biblical stories, dramatically different in mood as well as in use of color and medium. He has donated his complete works, more than a thousand paintings, to the museum and the city of Holstebro.

All art-minded tourists who visit Denmark want to see Louisiana, the museum located twenty miles north of Copenhagen. People are especially attracted by the beautiful setting in parklike, sculptured grounds and by the rambling architecture adapted to the terrain.

The museum was founded by businessman Knud Jensen, who ventured on his own to purchase the lovely old coastal property and remodel it into an exhibition center for modern art. (The name *Louisiana* is in tribute to an honored friend, architect Alexander Brun, who was married three times—each time to a Louise.)

Now partly supported by the government, Louisiana receives art donations from the Carlsberg Foundation, by whose statutes gifts may be made to state-supported museums. Exhibits include works of numerous sculptors and painters—many by the famous COBRA abstractionists. COBRA (*Co*penhagen, *Br*ussels, and *A*msterdam) was founded by Asger Jorn, Richard Mortensen, Henry Heerup, and Carl Henning-Pedersen.

Esbjerg Museum, located on the western coast of Jutland, exhibits some two hundred representative works by past and contemporary painters and sculptors whose names are familiar in the world of art. Included are those by the aforementioned COBRA artists, as well as contributions by Wilhelm Freddie, Olivia Holm, L. A. Ring, Sigurd Swane, Oluf Høst, Olaf Rude, and William Scharff, leader in the cubist movement.

Also displayed in the Esbjerg Museum is the lovely, realistic sculpture of an infant on a ball, *Nina paa Kuglen,* with arms outstretched. Of oxidized bronze, it occupies a prominent place in the museum. It is one of the best-known works by the renowned sculptor Kai Nielsen. His most famous piece is *Vandmoderen* (The Water Mother) from 1920.

In front of the museum stands a huge metal creation by modern iron sculptor Robert Jacobsen (born in 1912) of international fame. Jacobsen was one of the first to catch the spirit of the abstract sculpture movement in Denmark during the 1930s. Jacobsen's first items were small wooden pieces, mostly fantastic animals from fables. Later creations were of stone, and his latest and most successful have been those fashioned of iron and other metals. The expression of rhythm in lines and curves, as well as the fantasy of his lifelike figures, has given this artist a central place in twentieth-century art.

Denmark's contribution to the art of sculpture began with Johannes Wiedefelt (1731-1802), who brought back from Rome a taste for the antique and developed his own neo-classical style. His masterful hand executed the mourning figures of *Denmark* and *Norway* in marble for the tomb monument of Frederik V in Roskilde Cathedral and the sculptured figures for Fredensborg Castle Park.

But although Wiedefelt was the first of the classic sculptors, Bertel Thorvaldsen (1770-1844) was the artist who more nearly realized the ideals of the true classicist.

Thorvaldsen, a close friend of Hans Christian Andersen and the most renowned Danish classical sculptor, was born in a humble home in Copenhagen in 1770. Overcoming his father's objections to his study, Bertel entered the Royal Academy of Fine Arts, where he eventually took many awards, including a scholarship to study in Rome, the center of European art at that time. He left Copenhagen in 1797 and spent forty-one years in Rome, sculpting for princes, kings, and even the Pope. He also made numerous busts of famous personages, one hundred seventy-five in all.

In 1838, the Danish king sent a warship to Rome to escort Thorvaldsen home in style to Copenhagen, where a tremendous welcome awaited him. All his works accompanied him and were bequeathed to the city of Copenhagen. They are housed in the beautiful Thorvaldsen Museum, which was built soon after Thorvaldsen's return and is open to all today.

About ten miles from Helsingør, in an area that is rather barren and off the beaten path, lies an interesting museum devoted to the works of Rudolph Tegner and built by the artist himself. It contains all of his works in plaster, marble, and bronze—191 pieces of sculpture and 214 paintings—among them some mammoth and awesome works.

In the peaceful, private garden surrounding the museum, fifteen large sculptures stand in the Tegner Statue Park as a permanent memorial to the artist. One that has had many reproductions and one of the most charming is *The Thirsty Children*.

The Danes will tell you, "Even a beer glass is architecture (there is someting *in* that!)." If that is true, the field of architecture is too vast to be covered completely in a single section of this book.

The history of this art in Denmark can best be studied in person, for many castles, manors, churches, buildings, and homes have been refurbished by the state, and some of them are, in themselves, veritable museums. Entire villages in some areas have become state trusts and are saved for their historical interest.

From Denmark's smallest house in Ribe (three hundred years old)—so small it is more like a doll house—to a modern, experimental house made of plastic, the Danish house patterns are interesting to the student of photography as well as of architecture.

Nearly two thousand twelfth-century churches, including a few round fortress churches, provide a wealth of information through their frescoed paintings; while the Gothic cathedrals, like the one at Roskilde—the first and finest brick structure in Denmark—and St. Knud's Church in Odense, offer a course in Danish history as well as in early Danish architecture. One of the most unusual churches is the magnificent, five-towered fortress church in Kalundborg dating from A.D. 1170. The fortified and moated manor at Egeskov, the Renaissance Frederiksborg castle, and the baroque Fredensborg palace in northern Zealand are other structures that serve as examples of distinctive period design.

J. C. Krieger (1683-1755), one of the architects of

Fredensborg, was distinctly Danish in style, especially in his incomparable landscaped gardens, such as those still seen at Frederiksborg Castle, inspired by a blending of Italian and French design.

Architects Lauritz de Thura and Niels Eigtved strongly influenced the style of architecture in the early eighteenth century. Good examples are Thura's delightful Eremitagen, whose interiors are the best preserved baroque art in Denmark, and in Eigtved's Amalienborg Castle and Copenhagen mansions, often called the finest of their kind in Europe.

C. F. Hansen (1756-1845) inspired his followers by his exemplary structures, such as the former Christiansborg Castle, the town hall, and the courthouse in Copenhagen—none of which exist today. Martin Nyrup (1849-1921) carried out plans for the new city hall, now prominent in the city center. Best design of J. D. Herholdt (1818-1902) was the Copenhagen University Library, and greatest triumph of F. Meldahl (1827-1908) was the monumental Marble Church facing Amalienborg Square.

P. V. Jensen Klint won the design competition for the Grundtvig Church tower with the organ-like facade in 1913. His son, Kaare Klint, drew the plans for the building itself, consecrated in 1940—a combination of the typical village church and the Gothic town church.

Influenced by developments in Europe and America, international functionalism began to project itself into construction of all kinds in Denmark, including commercial structures like office buildings, stores, and factories, as well as into house plans. Simple, unconventional styles were introduced in row houses and housing developments—almost all of brick or stone. Extensive use of glass—unpretentious but practical—became the trend. Schools, city halls, athletic buildings—all began to acquire the new look in design.

Best known to students of architecture is Arne Jacobsen, who applied his talents to many fields, including designs for housing units, office buildings, factories, furniture, etc. In 1929, he was already a prizewinner for his House of the Future. The imposing twenty-two-story SAS Terminal and Hotel, so elegantly conspicuous in downtown Copenhagen, is of Jacobsen design—one of his earliest. He is also' well known for his circular, sun-rotating house in North Zealand, for the town halls of Århus and Søllerød, the Munkegaard secondary school, and the Novo Insulin Industry building—as well as numerous masterpieces of landscaping.

Possibly no other Scandinavian country is progressing as rapidly as Denmark in the building of new churches, even though church attendance has not kept up with this trend. Holger Jensen designed a number of churches built in the 1950s. The church at Rødovre is a notable example of his work. Jensen warned that churches, regrettably, have more to say about the people who created them than about God, and that the testimony might not be reversed until the churches were torn down.

In contrast to Jensen's observation is the noteworthy example of the inspired congregation of the Baptist church in Brande (Jutland) that conceived, planned, and built their own strikingly novel church. The final design was done by Kristian Kristiansen, but each member of the congregation brought a stone that became part of the used-brick front wall.

Whether the new Danish churches will stimulate church members to take a more active part is still a question, but the buildings are a dramatic departure from the traditional ecclesiastical architecture in an attempt to meet spiritual needs.

The circular-shaped Angli shirt factory, located on twenty-five acres near Herning in Jutland, has recently been acclaimed as an architectural first, both in design and efficiency. The building was conceived and planned by architect C. F. Møller of Århus and Professor C. Th. Sørensen of Copenhagen.

The name of Jørn Utzon (born in 1918) will be listed in the architectural annals of fame. In 1957, he won the international competition for the design of the spectacular opera house in Sydney, Australia. The building was officially opened in 1973, after fourteen years of construction. This masterpiece, as well as his museum in Silkeborg, will be a lasting tribute to Jørn Utzon and to Denmark.

The Danish inventor Karl Krøyer believes that changing family requirements and manufactured materials will transform architecture—possibly computerizing it—even to the building process. But he believes that will happen only when architects and builders become thoroughly emancipated from the traditional. Houses, he says, will never again be built to last for a hundred years or more, but will be more or less temporary, to be renewed or changed, like a person's wardrobe, to suit a fad- and fashion-conscious society.

Illustrating the experimental trend are two architects, Suzanne Ussing and her husband, Carsten Hoff, a couple of young, unrestricted Danish architects who constructed, in 1970, a house of tomorrow, made of light-weight steel pipes, brown wrapping paper, newspaper, ropes, and a reinforced transparent plastic foil.

Denmark has not isolated itself from international influences, for communication has facilitated the interchange of ideas. But even though standards of artistic quality may fluctuate with the times, Denmark will set for itself some independent standards that are based chiefly on the discovery of its own talents, appropriate media, and individual motifs, as it has done in the past. Denmark will continue to restore and preserve those arts and artifacts that are uniquely Danish, universally appreciated, and of timeless value.

The State Radio House and Symphony Hall
Insert: Composer Carl Nielsen

CHAPTER 19

MUSIC THAT LIVES

ON THE DANISH RADIO, a short melody is repeated again and again as an interval signal. Most people are surprised to learn that it is actually a remnant of the earliest recorded Danish music, dating back to a ballad found in manuscripts of the Scania Laws—about 1300. If Denmark has a distinctly national music, it may be based on the ballad, the old church modes, and the art song of the romantic period.

Apart from the ancient lays, Denmark's history of musical culture is not a long one. Its life, until comparatively recently, has been dependent on the contributions of foreign musicians —either visitors or permanent residents—or their influence from afar.

One of the best known Danish musicians is the monumental composer and organist, Diderik Buxtehude (1637-1707). Although Buxtehude spent most of his productive years in Germany, he began his magnificent career as organist in Saint Maria's Church in Helsingør, succeeding his father in that post. His beautiful cantata, "Let the Gates of Justice Be Opened unto Me," dates from this period.

As organist of the Marienkirche in Lübeck, Germany, where he served for two generations, Buxtehude expanded the performances to unheard-of proportions and succeeded in bringing music to the attention of the populace.

Among Buxtehude's works are thirty-nine organ compositions—preludes, fugues, toccatas—and fifty-four choral adaptations, many of which have been recorded. One reviewer has said, "Buxtehude's whimsicality and humor are Danish characteristics, more especially because they do not interfere with the logical sequence of the movement."

After Buxtehude died, there was a lull in Danish musical history. Several decades later, a genius arrived, Christopher Weyse (1774-1842), to provide a breakthrough for a national musical idiom—the true Danish ballad form.

It is significant that, although Weyse filled the prestigious post of organist at Our Lady's Church in Copenhagen for thirty-seven years and wrote many symphonies and dramatic works, his name is most often linked to a "people project." He set to music the beloved lyrics and religious poems of the great literary men of the Golden Age of Romanticism— for example, Oehlenschlaeger, Ingemann, Heiberg, Grundtvig, and Winther—and gave the people inspirational songs to sing.

Friedrich Kuhlau (1786-1832) was a contemporary of Weyse and, like him, a German by birth; but therewith ends the similarity of these two virtuosos. Kuhlau's most famous composition is a dramatic one, *Elverhøj,* based on Danish and Swedish ballad tunes plus textual material by Ewald and Heiberg. *Elverhøj* is said to be the most popular theater offering ever performed at the Royal Theater in Copenhagen. One of his lyrics is *Kong Kristian Stod ved Højen Mast,* the Danish royal anthem.

Two other musicians of this romantic period were related to each other by marriage—Niels W. Gade (1817-1890) and his father-in-law, Johan Hartmann (1805-1900).

Gade's success story reads almost like a fairy tale. An early composition, "Ossian Overture," was awarded a high prize by a Danish music association. (It is still heard in

Denmark.) The young composer received an even greater honor when his first symphony was performed in Leipzig, Germany. Returning to Denmark from Germany, Gade found himself practically king of music in Copenhagen. Almost immediately, he became organist at Holmens Church and director of the Royal Conservatoire. His most famous composition is *Elverskud,* still a popular concert-hall work.

Gade's father-in-law, Johan Hartmann, became organist at Our Lady's Church after Weyse's death and later served in high positions in musical organizations and at the Royal Conservatoire. Although he was an artist in several genres, he may be best remembered for the light-hearted opera and ballet *Liden Kirsten* (words by Hans Christian Andersen), on which Gade collaborated, or perhaps for the musical score for Oehlenschlaeger's "The Golden Horns" and other Nordic sagas.

In the late nineteenth century came Carl Nielsen (1865-1931). So great is the musical stature of Nielsen and so divergent his style, that one may classify all Danish composers as either pre-Carl Nielsen or post-Carl Nielsen. He is regarded as the father of modern Danish music.

This figure of international importance had a lowly birth in a peasant home near Odense, Funen. But although his parents were poor in worldly substance, they were rich in sensitivity and in love of music; and though Carl's home was simple, his surroundings on that lovely island were idyllic.

A story is told of Carl's first musical attempt. At age nine he was sick in bed with the measles. To divert him a bit, his mother gave him a small violin, which generally hung on the wall as an ornament. So familiar was the boy with the melodies he had heard his mother sing, that by playing with the little instrument, he could reproduce most of them by the time his father came home that evening. When the child played the songs for his parents, there was no comment; but his father took the violin, tuned it up to pitch, and returned it to the boy—for keeps.

Carl's youth was spent largely out of doors, for he was a cowherd. Much of his music reflects his childhood love for the beauties of nature, but there was another important experience in the artist's youth. He gained early contact with the folk high school and the Grundtvig movement—the cultural philosophy that stressed love of heritage and the importance of a religion of hope and happiness. These influences show up vividly in his music. His major contribution to Danish music, however, was his break with tradition —his use of innovative techniques.

In addition to several majestic symphonies, including *The Four Temperaments* and *Sinfonia Espansiva,* Nielsen wrote prolifically in other modes. There are, for example, his lovely chorale, *Hymnus Amoris;* the festival play, *The Mother;* a good deal of chamber music; and even delightful children's songs and stately hymns.

So numerous are the post-Carl Nielsen composers that it is almost impossible to make a capsular selection. But certain luminaries who are particularly Nordic as well as innovative can be singled out. For example, several of these modern composers have chosen literary or historical material as the theme for their compositions. Hakon Børresen's *The Love of a Mother* (on Hans Christian Andersen) and *Tycho Brahe* fall into this category. Peder Gram's *Prologue to a Shakespearian Drama*—popular both at home and abroad— has an obvious literary base, while Knud Jeppesen's *Queen Dagmar's Mass* uses the life of the beloved thirteenth-century queen as its text. Old Roman festivals form the central theme of Jørgen Bentzon's opera, *Saturnalia.*

The charming light opera, *Det Er Ganske Vist* (That Is

Quite True), written by Finn Høffding, is a cheerful Andersen story of a little, clucking hen who loses a feather and causes a scandal. Høffding's operas, *The Emperor's New Clothes* and *Kilderejsen,* are likewise adapted from popular stories by Andersen and Ludvig Holberg. There is also Ebbe Hamerik's *Variations on an Old Folksong Motif.* That's where the musical interval signal on Radio Danmark comes from.

The leading composer of the "new Danish music" may be the highly productive Niels Viggo Bentzon (born in 1919), although he has a number of close rivals, including Svend Tarp, Vagn Holmboe, Svend Schultz, Poul Olsen, Jan Maegaard, and Ib Nørholm.

One of the most famous modern performers in Denmark was Aksel Schiøtz, who died in 1975. Schiøtz, a tenor, was widely acclaimed as a recording artist. Internationally, he was famous for his performance of oratorios and the great song-cycles of Schubert and Schumann. However, to the Danes he was probably best beloved for his unique interpretation of Danish songs, notably those of Carl Nielsen.

Consider now some other aspects of Danish music. First, there is folk music and folksinging. This medium—once a great joy of the Danes—may be gradually disappearing from the scene, as it is throughout Europe, although attempts have been made to restore it through schools and festivals. For decades, in the late nineteenth and early twentieth centuries, it was almost impossible to keep folk songbooks in stock, so great was the demand for them. The tradition may well be revived.

One Danish musicologist, Nils Schiørring, has collected some hundred and fifty Danish folk and art songs within the repertoire of *one* singer—ballads, sea chanties, humorous ditties, and sentimental lyrics. And, fortunately, there are still many Danish people who can sing them with gusto and will pass them along to posterity.

Hymns in Denmark are different today. In fact, the change in hymns, begun by Carl Nielsen and Thomas Laub, has been the subject of much controversy. Thomas Laub was a leader in the restructuring of hymns from the romantic style to the modern, by making the melody subordinate to the words. The resulting enthusiasm and vehement objection still constitute a problem—a controversy similar to one in the United States over contemporary hymns.

The Danes really love music and, like Americans, begin to sing early in life. Children's songs compose a rich segment of Danish musical heritage, and schoolchildren delight in entertaining a visitor with their favorite songs.

Musical life in the provinces has been slow to mature. At least, it was underdeveloped until after World War II. Now, since the advent of radio and television and the help of generous government subsidies, it has begun to bloom.

Today there are eight distinguished professional symphony orchestras in Denmark. Four major ones have headquarters in Copenhagen—the Symphony Orchestra of Denmark's Radio, Zealand's Symphony Orchestra, Tivoli Orchestra, and the Royal Chapel Orchestra. Three are in the large provincial cities—Ålborg, Århus, and Odense; one is the South Jutland Orchestra. The Tivoli Symphony performs in the beautiful Tivoli Gardens during the summer and travels to southern Zealand and the smaller islands during the winter.

It is a credit to Danish culture that professional musical performances are not now limited to Copenhagen and the Royal Theater and Opera House. On many a special evening in one of the provincial towns, a large audience will pack the auditorium to capacity to hear a classical musical program performed by highly skilled artists.

Organs are a specialty of the Danes; in fact, Danish organs are among the finest in the world. The nation's four large organ-building firms send their custom-built instruments all over the world. It is natural that the Danes should appreciate and enjoy their own beautiful instruments and small wonder that they flock to such events as the annual international organ festival in the majestic Sorø Cathedral.

The proficient and comprehensive broadcasting system in Denmark has encouraged the expansion of musical activities throughout the nation. So have the courses offered at the universities and the music colleges, which now give professional training in music. Formerly, such study was available only at the Royal Conservatory in Copenhagen.

There is an interesting boys' music school in Copenhagen. This famous academy, called the Copenhagen Boys' Choir, was inaugurated in 1924. Boys nine years of age may audition for acceptance and receive not only regular academic work but also special musical training, particularly choral work, in both secular and sacred music.

Danish people seem to enjoy both the traditional and the new in music. Opera (sung in Danish) always brings out a large audience, as do orchestral and choral concerts. But chamber music concerts—by such distinguished ensembles as the Copenhagen String Quartet, the Danish Quartet, the Funen String Quartet, and the Prisma Ensemble—are special favorites.

What about "pop music" in Denmark? Without question, pop music plays an important role in the lifestyle of Danish youth. The "under-thirty set" tends to adopt the "in" thing of American and Danish pop music as relayed by radio and television and, like young people all over the world, to accept with enthusiasm the latest offerings of popular entertainers. At the same time, the young Danes—probably because of their Nordic sensitivity—like danceable, singable tunes and Western cowboy ballads. In fact, they like to sing while they dance.

Danes seem to have a special flair for rhythm. Often they can be seen walking arm in arm down the street, keeping precise step with barely audible band music (which they love) or humming a rhythmic melody together. They applaud in unanimous rhythm for good performances, considering that form of acclaim the most appreciative demonstration they can give.

The Danes are also a tuneful people, happy to express themselves—preferably corporately—in song and music. Spontaneous singing, with or without accompaniment, is the climax of any celebration, whether it be a graduation "fest" or a birthday party, a formal banquet or just a casual get-together. Certainly, one often hears the Danes joining their voices in one of their national anthems—especially their beloved *Der Er et Yndigt Land*.

The Danish people are musically creative, too. It is said, for example, that a certain popular ballad singer, Ingeborg Munch, makes up her best songs while milking her cow— and recommends the practice!

Even the Danish royalty sets the pace in musical creativity. The story is told of Prince Henrik, who was discovered one day seated at the organ of the Kai Munk Church in Jutland. An aide sat down and listened, perhaps a half hour or so, to the beautiful music. When the playing was over and the prince stepped down, the aide complimented the performance. "What was it you were playing, Your Majesty? I seem to recognize—uh, Bach or Beethoven—"

"No" replied Prince Henrik, "that was 'Improvisario' in the style of Henrik."

There is no one distinguishing feature of today's music

in Denmark. Variety is the keynote. Perhaps Danish music, like Danish literature, is in an era of exploration. How can musicians express their feelings psychologically and their theme artistically, use their Nordic heritage to advantage, select the best of the old mode and the best of the new, and still retain the simplicity and whimsicality so dear to the hearts of the natives?

Danish musicians may wish to search out a distinctive, national form. In the meantime, that little, recurring interval signal on the radio keeps reminding them, "We are Danes!"

The Royal Danish Ballet
Inserts: Ludvig Holberg
The Royal Theater

CHAPTER 20

THEATER, BALLET, AND OPERA

"THE VIKING FESTIVAL IS ON!"

Festive it is, indeed, at Frederikssund, the little village thirty miles north of Copenhagen in the Danish Riviera, when the annual play-pageant, *The Saga of Amled,* on which Shakespeare's *Hamlet* is based, is under way.

Picture the scene: It is early dusk. Huge buses full of tourists jockey for good parking spaces near the large outdoor amphitheater, as hundreds of automobiles pull up in between. Crowds begin pouring out to join pedestrians pushing toward the entrances to get the best seats on the wooden benches. All the while, loudly amplified medieval music is blaring. It is a carnival atmosphere.

As soon as everyone is seated—perhaps five hundred people in all—and the lights in the audience area begin to dim, a hush settles over the crowd. Dozens of torchlights appear out of nowhere to light up the enormous, natural stage, and gala participants in Viking dress rush on for their joyous opening scene—a royal welcome to a homecoming king. The ancient saga has begun.

Every summer since 1950, a cast of two hundred citizens of Frederikssund has performed this same handsome spectacular for a couple of weeks. While the play is given in Danish, it is easy for all to follow because of its familiar plot and its magnificent pageantry.

You can have a good time in the theaters of Denmark, especially if you visit during the theater season, which is, roughly, from September 1 to May 31. But there are also summer offerings like this Viking Festival in Frederikssund, the commedia dell'arte performances in the pantomime theater in Tivoli, and many other special events.

Tivoli, the world-famous amusement garden, located near the town square in Copenhagen, is always fun. It's also inexpensive. At certain times, the crowds drift in the direction of the music hall for the free concert of classical music, or, with the children, toward the large open amphitheater in the middle of the park—the pantomime theater. There all eyes are expectantly glued on the folding and unfolding peacock-tail stage curtain in anticipation of the show.

The summer of 1974 marked an unusually brilliant performance in Tivoli. On May 10, the mime theater celebrated its hundred-year jubilee, presenting the same commedia dell'arte repertoire given at its opening in 1874. All Tivoli— in fact, all Copenhagen—celebrated the event.

Copenhagen is the center of theatrical events. During the winter season seven or eight legitimate theaters are in operation (a drop of 50 percent from the 1950s), in addition to several avant-garde playhouses. But there are also excellent theater productions in the larger provincial towns—Århus, Odense, Ålborg, and Grenå—as well as locally produced theatricals in various places.

The national theater of Denmark is unique in that it is a four-part organization, incorporating not only the various kinds of drama but also the opera, the ballet, and the orchestra as well. Each of these four arts maintains a school of its own from which recruits are usually selected.

The present structure of the Royal Theater, located in Copenhagen's Kongens Nytorv, was one hundred years old in 1974. But the national theater as an organization goes back to 1748; in fact, it dates its initial opening to 1722, when the famous Ludvig Holberg began his flourishing dramatic career.

However, the history of Danish theatrical endeavor has not been all roses. Its darkest days came shortly after the opening of the Royal Theater in Copenhagen in September of 1722. The theater was totally destroyed by fire when much of Copenhagen was laid waste in 1795; and later, during the reign of Christian VI, it was closed by royal edict because pietism had become the dominant religion, and fun was frowned upon. However, when Frederik V succeeded to the throne in 1746, a new theater was built in Kongens Nytorv on the site of the present Royal Theater. Since that time, with only minor interruptions, that theater has presented a full season of plays each year from September through May, also sending out touring casts to perform in the provinces throughout Denmark.

In addition, numerous other national playhouses were established in Copenhagen as enthusiasm for live theater began to grow. They reached their highest popularity during the forties, fifties, and early sixties, when such playwrights as Soya, Rifbjerg, Munk, Erik Knudsen, and Ernest Olsen flourished. After this peak, theater attendance began to wane, presumably because of the popularity of radio and television drama.

In Århus, Ålborg, and Odense, enthusiasm for the legitimate stage seems to run high. Other provincial towns—such as Frederikssund, Sorø, Herning, Holstebro, and Grenå—have created their own theatrical offerings, some of which have escalated into a broader cultural program.

Sorø Academy in the town of Sorø gives an annual presentation of a Holberg play. Ludvig Holberg earned good money by sale of his plays, and because he was a thrifty bachelor, he accumulated considerable wealth. By the terms of his will, his property went to Sorø Academy, a boys' school, for its expansion and maintenance. Consequently, every year since Holberg's death in 1754 the academy has presented one of his comedies in honor of its illustrious benefactor.

By far the most innovative and revolutionary of the outlying theaters is the Odin Theater, established in 1966 in the Jutland town of Holstebro. The full name of this unusual drama center is the Odin Theater: Nordic Theater Laboratory for the Art of Acting. If you are a drama enthusiast—or even mildly interested in new art forms—you'll want to visit Holstebro, attend a performance, and get a firsthand look at one of the most widely discussed cultural experiments of the day.

The Odin group originally got together in 1964 in Oslo, Norway, under the leadership of a thirty-four-year-old Italian-born man, Eugenio Barba. Because of a successful Danish tour in 1966, the club was invited by the municipality of Holstebro (population 33,000) to pull up stakes in Norway and move to Denmark. The Holstebro city fathers offered the group an abandoned farm on which to set up location, and a stipend besides.

Since 1849, the Danish theater has been a state institution, underwritten by state funds and administered by the state through the Minister of Cultural Affairs. The Theater Law of 1970 made a number of changes that were generally of advantage to the entire field of drama and gave special support to theater in the more remote sections of the country and to children's theater, which has hit a new high in Denmark.

For example, there is a charming puppet theater which enlivens schoolchildren's field trips to the National Museum in Copenhagen. Here in the austere atmosphere of the old exhibition rooms, Denmark's Stone Age, Bronze Age, and Iron Age come to life through the antics of funny-looking puppet dolls, much to the merriment and enlightenment of the youngsters.

Other notable children's theaters which use puppets are Det Lille Teater, the traveling Comedievogn, and Abildstrøms Teater. Often the children themselves gleefully participate in the shows, especially after they have seen the plays a time or two.

The Danish theater today is keeping up quite well with its tradition of poetic creativity, in spite of considerable agitation within its ranks and deep concern over the obvious slump in attendance at legitimate playhouses. Playwrights, directors, designers, critics, and actors have combined their talents through the years to give the Danish public and their visitors a variety of enjoyable theatrical fare.

Whether visitors get a chance to see a revival of the delightful and popular *Kaerlighed uden Strømper* (Love without Stockings) or a performance of the mod and savage spoof on pop singers and the pop industry, *Teenager Love,* or any show at any of the places mentioned, they'll be getting something of the flavor of Danish theatrical ways.

A stage production at Tivoli may delight the audience with a portrayal of Queen Margrethe, Queen Elizabeth, and Henry Kissinger in a rollicking satire, or the Ridderhallen theater may depict characters from Shakespeare in hilarious situations. Takeoffs on famous personages are especially popular among the Danes.

While there is a growing segment of Danish youth embracing the "way out" theater, reflecting extremes of modern philosophy, chances are that the tourist will notice a predominance of light comedies and satires. For the most part, the typical Danish audience wants to laugh off its problems and enjoy itself at the theater. It loves to go out from the playhouse still chuckling over the jokes and funny situations, exclaiming, *"Jo, det var sjov!"* (Yes, that was fun).

And now the curtain rises on a performance of the Danish Royal Ballet during its annual festival held the first week in June at the Royal Theater in Copenhagen. The audience is hushed in anticipation, for what the eager ballet lovers are about to see is the finest exhibition of ballet dancing presented by the oldest ballet organization in the world.

Before the curtain goes up, people may have seen the motto *Ei Blot til Lyst* on the proscenium—a motto which expresses the feeling of most Danish theatergoers, as well as of performers, that "not just for pleasure" are they here, but for the appreciation and love of the art. For it is with a pride in perfection that the Royal Danish Ballet members— like the actors and opera stars on this stage—display their talents. They aim to live up to their reputation of presenting only the best material and expertly trained artists in each dramatic field.

The Danish Ballet dates back three hundred and fifty years, to the time it was first introduced in the courts of kings Frederik II, Christian IV, and Frederik III. Performances in the theater were begun in 1722, when the playhouse opened. In 1748 when the Royal Theater in Copenhagen was dedicated, the ballet began to attract foreign choreographers and performers as well as Danish ballet aspirants. In 1771, the Royal Danish Ballet was founded, and it has enjoyed an international reputation ever since.

Since 1966, Flemming Flindt, international guest performer and choreographer, has occupied the directorship of the Royal Ballet. Flindt has rewritten some of Eugene Ionesco's plays in collaboration with the author, producing several of his ballet dramas on television. His repertoire of works deviates somewhat from the classical dance pattern, and it appeals to the new young artists recruited from other countries. Two of his most recent ballets are *Dreamland* and *Dødens Triumf* (Death's Triumph). Both are accompanied by the Savage Rose, a Danish group of jazz singers, which is a major digression from the classic tradition, and takes its inspiration from the United States. In *Dødens Triumf,* the rock music gives a "mod" interpretation to the theme of death. All twelve episodes and thirty dancers portray a powerful drama of Life in confrontation with Death—in the frantic and earthy reactions of men and women to the inevitable and hopeless grip of doom. It is by no means a typically Danish ballet. The theme is a depressing one, and even though the first scene is hilariously funny, the Danish audience does not laugh at the attempt to introduce a tragedy by means of humor. Danes generally want humor that is broadly comical—not subtly satirical. However, internationally, and especially among young people, the production has been applauded.

The ballets of August Bournonville, who was director of the Royal Ballet in the late 1800s, have become popular in foreign—and especially American—ballet houses. Bournonville's ballets have always been those that challenge the outstanding solo performers in Denmark. Based on popular life as well as Danish history, the ballets are original, spiritual, and imaginative. Among his most renowned works are *Napoli* and *Danseskolen* (The Dancing School).

The first outstanding Danish prima ballerina of international note was Margot Lander, who retired in 1950. Among the many illustrious ballerinas who star in today's Royal Ballet are Kirsten Simone, Anna Laerkesen, Solveig Østergaard, and Mette Hønningen.

The male dancers in the Danish Ballet have been particularly acclaimed. Of outstanding talent and fame is Erik Bruhn, born in 1928, who trained under Lander and has been associated with many companies, including the American Ballet Theater. Other male artists, highly regarded on the national as well as international stage, are Henning Kronstam, Niels Kehlet, and Peter Martins.

The Danish Royal Opera has also existed in Denmark for more than a hundred and fifty years. It regularly presents works of Verdi, Mozart, Puccini, Strauss, and other composers, usually in Danish—to the delight of the Danish audiences. The Danish language, like Swedish, Italian, and French, is a musical tongue and lends itself well to the singing voice. The person who hasn't heard such operas as *Falstaff, Othello,* or *Der Fledermaus* sung in Danish, with Leif Roar, Niels Møller, and actor Henning Moritzen performing the leading roles, has missed a musical treat.

The first *Heldentenor* of the Viennese opera, regarded as one of the greatest heroic tenors of his day, was Eric Schmedes, who was born in Denmark. Lauritz Melchior, of American fame, is also claimed by the Danes, since he was born in Denmark and began his singing career there.

Operas are presented in most of the large cities of Denmark. In Århus, the second largest, nearly one hundred different operas have been given since 1947 in the splendid opera house. These have included works from nearly every well-known composer.

As the people leave the Royal Theater in Copenhagen after a thrilling performance of a ballet, opera, or play, they may glance up at the ceiling of the theater's beautiful mosaic arcade over the entrance and see a portrayal of the professions and activities of humankind surrounded by the significant words *Livet Er et Eventyr* (Life Is an Adventure). In thoughtful appreciation, they may stop to realize that the performing arts, through all of their varied and moving expressions, provide the ultimate in aesthetic experience for the public and the purest and most satisfying of adventures.

Danish contributions to the field of entertainment
in the U.S.
Inserts (left to right): Lauritz Melchior — Opera
Victor Borge — Stage
Jean Hersholt — Movies

Chapter 21

DANES IN THE UNITED STATES

MORE THAN A HUNDRED years ago, the first sizable group of Danes crossed the ocean, bound for the United States of America in search of new opportunities. The urge to migrate to the New World spread like a fever throughout Denmark, and hundreds of families pulled up stakes and set out for the far-off shores, most of them never to return.

Statistics show that nearly 362,000 men and women emigrated from Denmark to the United States between 1820 and 1972, but by far the largest number—312,000—between 1870 and 1929. In the single decade from 1881 to 1890, nearly ninety thousand individuals made the long, tiring journey, lured by the prospects of a better life and of streets paved with gold!

Danish immigrants scattered all over the United States in search of a new start in life. City-loving Danes settled in such metropolitan centers as New York, Chicago, Minneapolis, Omaha, and San Francisco, and took jobs in factories; while rural-oriented people selected farmlands, similar to Denmark's terrain, in Michigan, Illinois, Iowa, Wisconsin, Nebraska, and the Dakotas, and tilled the soil.

Most of the immigrants who were not indifferent to religion had been members of the established Lutheran Church in Denmark, but many of the early settlers were so busy keeping the wolf from the door that they found little time for church planning. The Elk Horn-Kimballton settlement in western Iowa was one of the notable exceptions. There, under the inspired leadership of theologian Kristian Anker (1848-1928), the church and school formed the focal point of the colony. For more than twenty years, Anker served as pastor of the large Danish congregation he had assembled and as president of the first folk high school in the United States. Under his administration, this school became an accredited normal school and college. The spiritual climate of this settlement was due, in large measure, to the influence of this beloved personage and the many inspiring and "fun" activities his ingenuity devised. On May 4, 1921, Pastor Anker was awarded the *Ridderkorset* (Knight's Cross) by Christian X for his outstanding leadership in Danish life in the New World.

Taking a cue from the Grundtvig philosophy of the importance of joy in religion and education, a score of folk high schools sprang up in various parts of the country after Elk Horn's leading venture. The longest lived one, in Solvang, California, lasted until 1937. While the Danish folk high schools no longer exist in the United States, the progressive educational concept is studied today and used as a popular model here and there, especially for summer school "short courses."

The Danish-American church was divided into two main factions—liberal *(Grundtvigsk)* and orthodox *(Indremissionsk)*—according to its prototype in Denmark. Both factions flourished and served well the religious segment of Danes in the United States—each synod having its own constitution, theological seminary and college, official newspaper, and, of course, church membership. Today the two church-based colleges are operating successfully as four-year liberal arts institutions and theological seminaries—Grand

View College in Des Moines, Iowa, and Dana College in Blair, Nebraska.

The numerous Danish churches in the United States have long since joined English-speaking Lutheran synods and have changed a good deal, both in doctrine and in format. A few of them still conduct occasional Danish services, and some continue to observe Danish customs of celebration, particularly at Christmas time.

The spirit of solidarity and mutual support among the Danes was of great help to those early settlers, both in the city and the country. Not only did the farmers cooperate on the work to be done, especially at times of illnesses and deaths, but people also gathered sociably, in stormy times and fair, to share their joys and sorrows, their advice and recipes. And they *sang*. How they loved to sing together— especially the folk songs and the hymns they knew so well!

But the relocation process was by no means all one of happiness for these immigrant men and women, who sometimes jokingly described themselves as creatures who stood astride—with one foot in Denmark and one in the United States. Stories ranging from general embarrassment and unkind "kidding" to acute suffering from homesickness, disasters, and gross injustice have come down to the second and third generations. Not least, of course, was the problem of the language barrier, which was a formidable hurdle.

Several factors besides the inspiration and fellowship of the church life helped to alleviate the difficulties of adjustment. One of these was the influence of the immigrant press; another was the morale-building activity of the fraternal lodges and other supportive organizations.

The Danish newspapers were a tremendous boon—especially when letters from Denmark began to taper off. And since the immigrant press printed highlights both from

Scandinavia and the United States, it served as a good Americanization medium as well as a comforting message from home.

The first Danish newspaper in this country was *Skandidinavia,* published in New York City in 1847. It was to have been a biweekly, but apparently only eight issues actually came out. Since that initial attempt, more than two hundred different Danish newspapers have been published in the United States. Most of them were comparatively short-lived, but some of them—like *Kirkelig Samler,* a church-based paper—ran for more than fifty years. The *Danish Pioneer*— a secular newspaper that was established in 1872—holds the record for the most subscribers and the longest life. *Kirke og Folk,* a church-oriented paper, and *Bien,* a San Francisco-based weekly, are also still in circulation.

Fraternal lodges were strong factors in providing sociability, cultural enrichment, and a means of adjustment to a new mode of living. One of the most active societies, still in operation today, is the Danish Brotherhood in America. With headquarters in Omaha, Nebraska, and lodges originally limited to four midwestern states—Nebraska, Iowa, Minnesota, and Wisconsin—the society expanded with astounding speed into all the northern states of the union— plus Florida. While it initially was an insurance society— and insurance is still its base—it gradually broadened to include a comprehensive program of activities, including college scholarships, old-age and unemployment assistance, cultural projects, and social gatherings. The brotherhood does a good job for its ten thousand members, now mostly descendants of Danish immigrants. Its official organ is *The American Dane.*

Headquarters of the Danish Brotherhood have remained in Omaha, in an attractive new building of Danish motif, even to the miniature tower on its roof—a small facsimile of the famous twisted dragon tails of the stock exchange tower in Copenhagen. It is the only building in the United States, except perhaps the Danish embassy, where *Dannebrog* and the Stars and Stripes fly side by side each day of the year.

The history of the American-Scandinavian Foundation in New York City and its current activities would require a volume in itself. But one of its divisions, the Danish American Women's Association, should be mentioned here. It was a strong supportive force for philanthropy and cultural enrichment among Scandinavian immigrants. This association was established in 1928 to help the poor and sick among Danish Americans and to promote in the United States an appreciation of the Danish cultural heritage.

Another interesting society, that of the Danish Royal Guards in Foreign Lands, is a select group composed exclusively of men who were members of the Danish royal guard in their youth and who wish to keep in touch with their compatriots in Denmark. When Jørgen Hansen, a member of this organization, celebrated his one-hundredth birthday on May 18, 1975, in Eugene, Oregon, he received a congratulatory letter from Queen Margrethe herself.

The Danes were eager to become good American citizens. Some went overboard in those early days of relocation by renouncing or denying their Scandinavian heritage, but most of them probably achieved a cultural blend of sorts and learned to serve loyally their adopted country both in peace and war. Their reputation for integrity and ability earned them the respect of their American friends.

In the New York Historical Library there is a biographical index, written by Baron Joost Dahlerup, about some forty thousand Danes in the United States. From that volume one might select a *long* list of illustrious men and women, who have not only adapted well to their new country but have brought it, as well as Denmark, remarkable distinction. Consider here only a few, chosen from various fields of achievement.

Jacob Riis (1849-1914) was a friend to underlings in American society—"life's stepchildren," as he called them. His book, *How the Other Half Lives* (1899)—the first of a series on slum life in New York City—his numerous articles and lectures, plus his friendship with President Theodore Roosevelt, helped to bring about many social reforms.

Several American Christmas traditions were started by Jacob Riis, including the custom of caroling on Christmas Eve, the use of the word Yule for Christmas, and setting up a municipal Christmas tree (New York City set up its first tree in Madison Square in 1912 at Riis' suggestion). The Red Cross Christmas seal used by the National Tuberculosis Association was adopted because of Riis' influence (six of his brothers had died of tuberculosis).

Film star and philanthropist Jean Hersholt was a Danish American. His greatest fame may lie in his portrayal of *The Country Doctor,* though he played, in all, some four hundred fifty other roles and three times received an Oscar for acting. He is famous, too, for his translation of Hans Christian Andersen's works—begun in 1939—publishing a total of a hundred thousand copies—and for his gift collection of first editions to the Andersen Museum in Odense and duplicates to the Library of Congress.

Knighted Lauritz Melchior became interested in opera when he used to take his blind sister to a seat near the stage reserved for the blind, but he never really "saw" an opera till he appeared in one. In 1946 he celebrated his twenty-year jubilee at the New York Metropolitan Opera House.

He sang the same title role he had sung there in 1926—in Wagner's *Tannhauser*.

In Central Park, New York City, on September 18, 1957, a fine bronze statue of Hans Christian Andersen was unveiled and dedicated to children's enjoyment in the presence of fifteen hundred persons. Located in one of the park's prettiest areas, it has become a popular story-telling center. Originator of the seventy-five-thousand-dollar project was Baroness Alma Dahlerup, first woman to receive the Danish award, *Ridderkorset,* as well as other high honors, for her distinguished service, chiefly through her long-term post as president of Danish American Women's Association, which she also founded.

Another philanthropist was the famous organ builder Mathias P. Møller, who also was a recipient of *Ridderkorset.* Møller began work as a poor immigrant boy, learned the organ-building craft, and founded in Philadelphia the highly successful organ factory that bears his name. His son, M. P. Møller, Jr., took over the factory after his father's death. Møller organs, of which the senior organ builder built sixty-five hundred during his lifetime, are considered among the finest in the world.

International lawyer and judge Fred K. Nielsen, born in Slagelse on Zealand, sat at the Peace Table in Versailles in 1918. As Solicitor of State under Woodrow Wilson and appointee to international posts under every president from Wilson to Eisenhower, he represented the United States in numerous court cases. For his achievements he was awarded honorary doctoral degrees from the University of Nebraska, his alma mater, and Georgetown University, where he was professor of international law.

Scandinavian festivals in the United States are delightful reminders of the culture and contributions of the Danish people. Though there are a number of these celebrations held annually in various American towns, four have attracted special attention—one at Junction City, Oregon; one at Solvang, California; one at Greenville, Michigan; and one at Minden, Nebraska.

The Junction City annual event began in 1960 as a family fun fest for the enjoyment of the town's many Scandinavian citizens, and it is now attracting hundreds of visitors from all over Oregon and elsewhere. Early in August the decorated booths, displays, and festooned flags go up almost overnight in the streets of the small town, and people don their authentic Scandinavian costumes for the four-day event, one day of which is designated as especially Danish. A gala spirit prevails all four days.

The same sort of atmosphere delights visitors at Solvang, California, especially during their Danish Days celebration in September. However, there is an old world charm in Solvang all the year around, as Solvang (Sunny Vale) dates back to its founding by Danish educators and their folk high school in 1911. Solvang's all-Danish motif in architecture has been greatly enhanced since World War II. Cross-beamed walls in houses and stores, tile or thatched roofs, stretches of cobblestone sidewalks, stork figures on the chimney tops, prim gaslights here and there, and a windmill or two give the town an authentic Danish feeling.

Greenville, Michigan, one of the oldest Danish settlements, has a Danish fair in the middle of August to perpetuate the customs, folklore, and lifestyle of the American Dane. Minden, Nebraska, celebrates in June.

The time was—a generation or so ago—when many a Dane tried to conceal his identity. Not so today. Today, when Danish furniture, Danish porcelain, Danish silver, Danish sandwiches, Danish education, and Danish festivals are things to buy and enjoy and emulate, only the foolish Danes will hide their heritage.

It is as if the countless Danes—and those of Danish ancestry—so long possessed by the desire to become completely absorbed into the melting pot of America, are now responding to a revival of ethnic identity and are regaining a pride in their heritage. And well they might! It is a worthy heritage.

> *Maalt med verden er det lille,*
> *derfor ingen plet at spilde;*
> *maalt med hjaertet er det stort;*
> *der er Danmarks saga gjort.*
>
> In the larger world, she is very small,
> so wasted is no spot at all;
> As to her heart, as large as gold,
> therein is Denmark's saga told.

ACKNOWLEDGMENTS

THE AUTHORS WISH TO THANK all those who have helped immeasurably in furnishing information for the writing of this book. Our sincere thanks to Pastor Johannes Langhoff, assistant to the bishop of Copenhagen and representative to the World Council of Churches; Gunnar Stig, editor, Information Department, Danfoss Industry, Nordborg, Denmark; Poul Lyngby, International Office, Ministry of Education, Copenhagen; Dr. Pieben Ollendorff, Director of Internal Medicine, Landshospitalet, Sønderborg, Denmark; Drs. K. O. Christensen, Peter Kjaer, Poul Black, and F. Gyentenberg, Copenhagen; Axel Skelbeck, former national executive secretary of Danish Brotherhood in America, Omaha, Nebraska; Mr. and Mrs. Johannes Hansen, Løvemose Ceramics, on Langeland Island; the Eivand Hjulmand family, Ålborg, Denmark; the Søren Nielsen family, Springkildegaard, Tvingstrup, Denmark; Birte and Per Skanderby, and Birgitte and David Nelson, Nordenfjord World University, northern Jutland, Denmark; and Mr. and Mrs. Karl Johann Villadsen, Braband, Denmark.

We also extend our appreciation to the various official offices from which we secured informational material, including the International Office, Socialministeriet, Copenhagen, Denmark; Danish Sports Federation, Glostrup, Denmark; and Scanticon in Tønder, Denmark.

Credit is also hereby given to Piet Hein, who gave permission for the use of three poems from: *Grooks,* Doubleday and Co., Inc., Copyright Aspila, 1970.

We also wish to thank the numerous teachers, museum directors, pastors, librarians, tour leaders, and friends with whom we spoke informally. Our warmest gratitude goes to author MacHaffie's husband, Dr. R. A. MacHaffie, for his excellent help in research and evaluation.

CASTLES

IF YOU VISIT DENMARK, you'll find an interesting and historic castle at almost every turn. Here are twelve of the most famous ones. You won't want to miss them!

Nyborg Castle, on the eastern coast of Funen, is the oldest, best-preserved castle to be found in Scandinavia. Built in 1170, it is picturesquely situated at the entrance to the Store Belt. In this castle, in 1282, King Erik Klipping drew up the first Danish constitution, the Great Charter. From that year until 1413, the *Danehof,* or first council, composed of clergy and nobles, met there regularly. King Christian II was born in Nyborg Castle in 1481, and during his reign he decided to add another wing and tower of imposing Renaissance design to the structure. Much of what he built still remains intact and is open to the public as a museum.

Vordingborg Castle in southern Zealand was built in the 1300s as a home for Margrethe, the daughter of Valdemar IV. It also was planned as a fortress to protect southern Denmark. Only the Goose Tower of the castle remains today. The "goose" supposedly was screeching resolution and defiance against the Germans to the south.

Gjorslev Castle, south of Copenhagen, was the only castle Margrethe I permitted to be built during her reign. Located just past Magleby, it was erected in the early 1400s for the Bishop of Roskilde. It is the only Danish castle still standing that was constructed in the once-popular shape of the Greek cross.

During the reign of Eric of Pomerania (1412-1439), the ramparts at Kronborg in Helsingør, on the Kattegat, were built in order to collect tolls from ships passing through the Sound. *Kronborg Castle,* of Hamlet's fame, was later constructed on the site by King Frederik II. Built during the sixteenth century and greatly damaged by fire in 1629, it was later restored and used as a barracks from 1725 to 1924. Then it was remodeled as a museum and opened to the public.

Rosenholm Castle, home of the Rosenkrantz family, was built in Jutland in the sixteenth century by Jørgen Rosenkrantz, and the estate still belongs to that family. The name bears much weight and is well thought of in Danish history.

Rosenholm Castle is one of the few remaining four-towered citadels from that time. Like other Danish castles, it contains many royal portraits as well as lovely furnishings and tapestries.

Not far from Viborg in Jutland lies *Spøttrup Castle,* a stark brick structure with only a few windows, built during the fifteenth century and once the property of the Bishop of Viborg. One of the most impressive of castles, it has been greatly restored and still has heavy ramparts and a moat with a drawbridge. The Knights' Hall has been reconstructed, but unchanged are the lovely baroque rooms on the first floor.

Built about 1550 is *Egeskov Castle,* perhaps the loveliest of old castle estates, lying just off the Fåborg Highway, not far from Knaerndrup, in Funen. A familiar-looking windmill is seen at the approach to the manor; it is the one that appears on the Danish ten-kroner note. The magnificent, stately castle, with its large corner towers and central tower built for defense, seems to rise right out of the lake in which it is reflected. It is said that an entire forest of oak trees was used to provide the twelve hundred piles driven into the mud on which the castle is built.

Rosenborg Palace is one of the most interesting museums in Europe. Christian IV, who reigned from 1588 to 1648, personally supervised the building of this palace. Situated only a short distance from the city hall in Copenhagen, it was built as a summer residence for the royal family on a tract of land which was then outside the city limits. The three-storied brick building is ornamented with perforated turrets of varied shape and height, extending 65 to 160 feet above the roof. Inside the castle, the history of Denmark is vividly depicted by magnificently painted walls and ceilings, and by the vast collection of treasures and relics. On the top floor, in the Knights' Hall, is the king's throne of sea ivory with three silver lions. The precious crown jewels are on this floor, electrically guarded in a glass-sealed case. If the case is touched, it will disappear into the basement below and set off a series of alarms. The royal crowns, necklaces, scepters, and kingly regalia ornamented with gold, pearls, and diamonds bring gasps from the thousands of viewers who stop to admire the royal gems.

The greater part of *Frederiksborg Castle,* one of the most beautiful pieces of Renaissance architecture in Scandinavia, was another of the masterpieces wrought by King Christian IV. It is named after Christian's father, Frederik II. Spectacularly dominating the landscape in a lovely wooded setting overlooking a lake in northern Zealand, the castle was the favorite residence of the kings of Denmark for nearly two hundred years. It was the scene of many coronations and royal celebrations.

Most of the building was destroyed by fire in 1859, and only the thick walls and the interiors of the chapel and the audience chamber were saved. Although the castle was partially restored by the royal family, complete reconstruction was the work of the founder of the Carlsberg Breweries, J. C. Jacobsen, who offered to finance the establishment of a historical museum within the castle. This monumental castle museum, opened in 1884, houses extensive collections relating to all aspects of Denmark's colorful history.

During the latter part of Christian IV's reign, *Gyldensten Castle* was built a few miles east of Bogense, a city on Funen, by the builder Gryns Krabbe, whose initials are seen on the wrought iron gable of one of the farm buildings. Later, when the castle and grounds became a *grevskab,* or county seat, its owner was created Count of Gyldensteen. It later came to be owned by the Bernstorff family, descendants of Andreas Peter Bernstorff, who, as Prime Minister in 1788, freed the Danish peasants from feudal law.

Built around an enormous court, the half-timbered barns and stables with thatched roofs almost hide the castle, lying behind a moat-covered bridge bounded by lime trees.

Fredensborg (meaning Peace Castle) is an example of Frederik IV's taste for the Italian style in architecture. It commemorates the 1720 peace treaty with Sweden. This lovely palace, set in a semi-secluded area and banked by tree-lined avenues leading toward it, does indeed inspire a feeling of peace.

Architecturally, Fredensborg is known for its lofty, domed hall and magnificently painted ceilings, also characteristic of Clausholm Castle. Later it became the favorite home of Christian IX, "the father-in-law of European royalty," as the location for large family reunions, which included half the crowned heads of Europe, seventy or more relatives by birth or marriage. Today the castle is used by Denmark's royal family every autumn.

Copenhagen Castle, for more than three hundred years Denmark's royal residence and center of historical events, had been completely refurbished in the 1720s by Frederik IV, father of Christian VI. But it was promptly torn down by his son, Christian, when he became king, and on the site the first of three structures known as *Christiansborg Castle* was constructed. (Eight hundred years earlier, on this spot overlooking the harbor, Bishop Absalon had erected his fortress home, sections of which you may still see around the present castle.) Christian VI's baroque-styled edifice was destroyed by fire in 1794. The second castle, of neo-classic design, was dedicated in November 1828, during the reign of Frederik VI. Later, in 1849, it was in this castle that *Grundloven,* the first liberal constitution for Denmark, was signed.

In spite of the many precautions that had been taken to prevent another disastrous fire, the second Christiansborg was destroyed by flames on October 3, 1884.

It was not until 1903, during the fortieth anniversary of the reign of King Christian IX, that the building of a third Christiansborg Castle was undertaken. King Frederik VIII laid the cornerstone for the present structure on November 15, 1907. The stone, which had been removed from the foundation of Absalon's house, was inscribed with the three words *Rex, Lex,* and *Jus* to symbolize that the castle was built to house the country's highest governmental authorities—the king, the parliament, and the courts. Today Christiansborg is no longer a royal residence or a judicial building, but it houses the parliament and serves as a museum as well.

DANISH SONGS

SONGS THAT ARE STILL SUNG by all Danes, young and old today, include the morning song written by the composer Christopher Weyse, with words by the famous Danish poet and novelist, B. S. Ingemann:

> *I østen stiger solen op;*
> *den spreder guld paa sky,*
> *gaar over hav og bjaergetop,*
> *gaar over land og by.*

> *Den kommer fra den fagre kyst,*
> *hvor Paradiset laa;*
> *den bringer lys og liv og lyst*
> *til store og til smaa.*

The sun arises in the east,
it gilds the heavens wide,
and spreads its light on mountain peak,
on town and countryside.

It rises from the distant shore
where Paradise began;
brings life and joy forever more
to every child and man.

Nu titte til hinanden de favre blomster smaa,
de muntre fugle kalde paa hverandre;
nu alle jordens børn deres øjne opslaa,
nu sneglen med hus paa ryg vil vandre.

The fresh morning flowers now are peeking from their beds,
and cheerful birds are whistling to each other;
as all the young on earth now raise up their tiny heads,
the snail, house on his back, will wander further.

Julen har bragt velsignet bud,
nu glaedes gamle og unge,
hvad englene sang i verden ud,
nu alle smaa børn skal sjunge;
grenen fra livets trae staar skønt
med lys som fugle paa kviste,
det barn, som sig glaeder fromt og kønt,
skal aldrig den glaede miste.

Christmas has brought its blessings again,
now old and young are rejoicing.
The message of peace which angels sang,
all children with joy will be voicing.
On branches the tree of life is bright
with lights, like birds, giving pleasure.
All children, whose joy is pure and right,
their joy forever will treasure.

The following stanzas are also by Ingemann:

Fred hviler over land og by,
ej verden larmer mer,
fro smiler maanen til sin sky,
til stjaerne stjaerne ser.

Fred med hvert hjaerte fjaern og naer,
som uden ro mon slaa!
fred med de faa, som mig har kaer,
og dem, jeg aldrig saa.

Peace hovers o'er the countryside,
the world from noises flees;
the moon smiles sweetly in its sky,
each star a star perceives.

Peace to each heart both far and near,
which beats in restless woe;
Peace with the few whom I hold dear,
and with those I do not know.

Here is a lullaby, *"Laer Mig, Nattens Stjerne"* by Christian
Richardt:

Laer mig, nattens stjerne,
at lyde fast og gerne!
Ej at vige fra den vej
Himlens Gud tilmaalte mig!
Laer mig, nattens stjerne!

Laer mig, markens blommer
at bie paa min sommer,
midt i verdens dybe ve
at spire under vintersne!
Laer mig, markens blommer!

Laer mig, golde hede,
du brune laerkerede,
nøjet med en fattig høst
at huse sangen ved mit bryst!
Laer mig, golde hede!

Sol i Aftensvale,
laer mig den kunst at dale!
Kun mod nattens dyb at gaa
for nyfødt atter at opstaa!
Laer mig, sol, at dale!

Evening star up yonder,
Teach me like you to wander
willing and obediently
the path that God ordained for me.
Evening star up yonder!

Teach me, gentle flowers,
to wait for springtime showers,
in this winter world to grow
green and strong beneath the snow.
Teach me, gentle flowers!

Teach me, lonely heather,
where songbirds nest together,
though my life should seem unblest,
to keep a song within my breast.
Teach me, lonely heather!

Evening sun, descending,
teach me, when life is ending,
night shall pass and I, like you,
shall rise again, where life is new!
Teach me, sun descending!

This song, entitled *"Danmark, Mit Faedreland,"* written by Hans
Christian Andersen in memory of his native Fyn, has become
one of Denmark's best-loved national songs:

I Danmark er jeg født, der har jeg hjemme,
Der har jeg rod, derfra min verden gaar.
Du danske sprog, du er min moders stemme,
Saa sødt velsignet du mit hjerte naar.

Du danske friske strand,
Hvor oldtids kjaempegrave
Staar mellem aeblegaard og humlehave,
Dig elsker jeg! — Danmark, mit Faedreland!

Engang du herre var i hele Norden,
Bød over England — nu du kaldes svag,
Et lille land, — og dog saa vidt om jorden
End høres Danskens sang og meiselslag;
Du danske friske strand, —
Plovjernet guldhorn finder.
Gud, giv dig fremtid, som han gav dig minder,
Dig elsker jeg! — Danmark, mit Faedreland!

In Denmark I was born, and there 'tis homely,
there clings the root whence all my being flows.
O Danish tongue, your tones are soft and comely,
none but a mother's voice could soothe like those.
            You smiling Danish strand,
                  where Viking barrows muster,
while round them orchards bloom and hop-vines cluster
'tis you I love — Denmark, my native land!

You mastered England once and overran it,
ruled all the North — but now men say you wane;
so small a land — yet up and down our planet
still ring the song and chisel of the Dane.
            You smiling Danish strand,
                  plough turns up golden treasure;
God gild your future, too, in equal measure!
'tis you I love — Denmark, my native land!

Appendix C

COMMON EXPRESSIONS AND SIGNS

When driving a car:

Højst ..... maximum speed
Højre .... to the right
Venstre .... to the left
P .... parking lot or rest area
Parkering forbudt .. parking forbidden
Ensrettet (with arrow) one way
Omkørsel .... detour
Indkørsel .... entrance
Udkørsel .... exit
Ingen indgang ... no entrance
No right turn on a red light in Denmark!

Personal:

Herrer .... men's rest room
Damer ... women's rest room
(Be careful, though, not to say "Dame Hansen!")
Frue .... Mrs.
Frøken .... Miss
Lukket .... closed
Aaben .... open
Optaget .... occupied
Nedgang .... stairway down
Opgang .... stairway up
Selv-betjening ... self-service
Frisør .. *(Dame frisør)* beauty parlor
Herre frisør .... barber shop

Eating and Shopping:

Morgenmad ..... breakfast
Frokost .... lunch
Middag .... dinner
Smørrebrød ..... open-faced sandwich
Soda vand ...... soft drink
Øl .... beer
Spisekort .... menu
Pris .... price
Regningen .... the bill
Is .... ice cream
Pølser .... hot dogs
Kiosk .... newsstand
Bageri .... bakery
Mejeri ..... dairy (milk and cheese)
Slagteri ...... meat market
Købmand ..... grocery store
Brugsen .. grocery chain store
Renseri .... cleaners
Konditori .... bakery goods and delicatessen
Blomster .... flowers

Miscellaneous:

Bil .... car
Biler .... cars
Børnehaven .... day nursery
Havnen .... harbor
Lufthavnen .... airport
Dyner ...... feather quilts
Døgn .... 24 hours
Fjernsyn .... television
God .... good
Gods .... baggage
Køligt .... cool
Varmt .... warm
Skole .... school
Worth knowing: When making a telephone call, *Indkast 1 x 5 kr.* means "Insert one kr. at a time to a total of 5 kr."

SELECTED BIBLIOGRAPHY

Almgren, Bertil, et al. *The Viking*. New York: Crescent Books, 1972.

Andersen, Willy. *Ser Man Det* (II). Aalborg: SV Press a/v, 1974.

Barhache, Jean. *Denmark*. London and New York: Vista Books, 1960.

Bauditz, Sophus, ed. *H. C. Andersen's Eventyr og Historier*. Copenhagen: Gyldendalske Boghandel, 1905.

Bjørnsen, Mette Koefoed, and Hansen, Erik. *Facts about Denmark*. Copenhagen: Politikens Forlag, 1972.

Boesen, Gudmund. *Danish Museums*. Copenhagen: Committee for Danish Cultural Activities Abroad, 1966.

Clark, Sydney. *All the Best in Scandinavia*. New York: Dodd, Mead, 1968.

Denmark, An Official Handbook. Copenhagen: Royal Danish Ministry of Foreign Affairs, 1970.

Dennis-Jones, H. *Your Guide to Denmark*. New York: Funk and Wagnalls, 1969.

Griffin, G. W. *My Danish Days*. Philadelphia: Claxton, Remsen, and Haffelfinger, 1875.

Halmundsen, Hallberg, ed. *An Anthology of Scandinavian Literature*. New York: Collier, 1965.

Hürlimann, Martin, and Oxenstjerna, Eric. *Scandinavia*. New York: Viking, 1967.

Innes, Hammond. *Scandinavia*. New York: Time, 1962.

Jansen, F.; Billeskov, J.; and Mitchell, P. M., eds. *Anthology of Danish Literature*. Carbondale: Southern Illinois University Press, 1971.

Jones, W. Glyn. *Johannes Jørgensen*. New York: Twayne, 1969.

Kappel, Vagn. *Danish Composers*. Copenhagen: Det Danske Selskab, 1967.

Larsen, Hanna Astrup, ed. *Denmark's Best Stories*. New York: The American-Scandinavian Foundation, Norton, 1928.

Laurin, Carl; Hannover, Emil; and Thiis, Jens. *Scandinavian Art*. New York: American-Scandinavian Foundation, 1922.

Nörlund, Paul; Struckmann, Erik; and Swane, Leo, eds. *Danish Art Through the Ages*. Copenhagen: Tidskriftet, 1948.

Oakley, Stewart. *A Short History of Denmark*. New York: Praeger, 1972.

Old Stories from Denmark. Illustrated by Poul Lundsgaard. Ebeltoft, Denmark: Elles Boghandel, n.d.

Oxenstjerna, Eric. *The Norsemen*. Translated by Catherine Hutter. New York: New York Graphic Society, 1965.

Polomé, Edgar C., ed. *Old Norse Literature and Mythology*. Austin, Texas: University of Texas Press, 1969.

Scandinavia. Fodor's Modern Guides. New York: McKay, 1966.

Siegner, Otto. *Scandinavia—Denmark, Sweden, Norway*. New York: Scribner, 1971.

Sitwell, Sacheverell. *Denmark*. London: B. T. Batsford, Ltd., 1956.

Stork, Charles Wharton, trans. *A Second Book of Danish Verse*. Freeport, N. Y.: Books for Libraries Press, 1968.

Strode, Hudson. *Denmark Is a Lovely Land*. New York: Harcourt Brace, 1951.

Williams, Alan Moray. *Denmark, Praise and Protest*. Copenhagen: Høst og Sons Forlag, 1969.

Wuorinen, John H. *Scandinavia—The Modern Nations in Historical Perspective*. Englewood Cliffs, N. J.: Prentice-Hall, 1965.

INDEX